DAYS OF GLORY

Days of Glory

*The Passion, Death, and Resurrection
of Jesus Christ*

Richard T.A. Murphy, O.P.

Servant Books
Ann Arbor, Michigan

2 0 2

232.96
M 978d

CONTENTS

CHAPTER ONE

The Passion of Jesus

Jesus of Nazareth is the most fascinating, mysterious, and important person the world has ever seen. In the course of time there have been many famous men and women, most of whom are at best vaguely remembered, and many entirely forgotten. Jesus Christ, by contrast, is very much alive.

The attraction he exercises over men has nothing to do with family connections or his native land. His family had seen better days, and his land was a tiny strip along the eastern shore of the Mediterranean, of no particular resources or value except as a land bridge between Mesopotamia and Egypt. The man himself is the spell. His message, everywhere and always, was the approaching kingdom of God. "No man ever spoke as this man speaks," was the verdict of his contemporaries. Besides that, there was his mastery over demons and unclean spirits, his ability to heal all sorts of sickness, his miracles (some of them dramatic, others simply performed), his serenity and mental alertness in the midst of hostile foes, his steadfast devotion to a mission that brought him to his death. But even in death he is unusual; his story, instead of ending at the tomb, really begins there. He alone of all mortal men rose from the dead to live forever.

Countless books have been written about Jesus in an effort to penetrate the veil of mystery that surrounds him. It is no longer fashionable to write "lives of Jesus" (the gospels do not provide enough information for this), but each book is a tribute

1

to him. He has recently been "discovered" by the motion pictures and television. With the exception of Zeffirelli's *Jesus of Nazareth* and, in a less devout way, Jewison's *Jesus Christ Superstar*, he has not fared well in the communications media, which depict him as a one-dimensional and distant character no one could relate to. How could they? He never smiles, never sweats, and never relates to people as if he knew what it is like to be the human beings he has come to save. People cannot relate to a plastic figure of a man, but they have always related to the Jesus in the gospels. The gospels are still our best and practically our only source of information about him.

God's plan for man's salvation was sketched out in the Jewish scriptures. It was not to be carried out by divine fiat but by the sufferings of one of his servants. Christians call him the Messiah, God's Anointed One, or simply, the Christ. He had long been awaited, and the Chosen People had seen his picture emerge from the pages of their sacred books. It was a picture that was never to achieve photographic clarity, but it was clear enough to fire an intense hope. The Messiah would be victorious over the powers of evil—a breathtaking promise that was first made in the garden of Eden just when it seemed that God's gracious plan for mankind had been sabotaged (Gn 3, esp. v. 15). It was later perceived that this person would be a prophet like Moses, and a descendant of David. He would not be a priest according to the ancient order of Aaron, but of that of Melchisedech. He was to establish an enduring kingdom. This mysterious figure was priest, prophet, and king, and there were intimations of universality too: his dominion was to extend over all men and all the world.

These ancient writings presented the Messiah in a curious combination of light and shadow. The great Isaiah told of a suffering servant who was to be an expiatory victim for sins, and his account (ch. 53) reads almost like a fifth gospel. The prophet Zechariah spoke of one whose side had been pierced, a shepherd valued at a miserable price of thirty silver pieces (Zec 12:10; 11:13), and the Psalmist (Ps 22) spoke eloquently of one "forsaken" by God.

The mystery of the cross is, as St. Paul said (1 Cor 1: 23), to the Jews a stumbling block, and an absurdity to the Gentiles. Jewish thinkers stubbornly resisted the idea of a suffering Messiah. Their Messiah was to restore Israel's glory. Oppressor nations would feel his wrath, and all Israel would share in his triumph. Scriptural passages which in any way linked the Messiah with suffering were consistently applied either to the Temple (more than once profaned in its history), or to the Jewish people. Thus there came into being the idea of a collective Messiah. The concept of an individual, suffering Messiah who expiated for the sins of others, is a distinctively Christian contribution to the history of salvation.

Our aim in these pages is to provide a better appreciation of the passion, death, and resurrection of Jesus. The text will be allowed to speak for itself. The story has its own impact, and we shall try not to interfere with it. The project is not without difficulty. Scholarly debates circle endlessly about details. Theories popular one day are forgotten the next. These theories are not without importance, since human knowledge is often advanced by fits and starts. However, a paragraph of any biblical author is not one whit improved by being labelled this or that kind of story. Chronological difficulties exercise a fascination for the historian, but such considerations—also not without importance—are in fact for the most part peripheral. Dodd put it well when he pointed out that the duty of the interpreter is to see what he can do with the text as it has come down to us, before attempting to improve upon it (*The Fourth Gospel*, p. 290). That is an acute observation. The reliability and inspiration of the text is vouched for by the Church, and common sense would suggest that nothing really earthshaking is likely to be discovered about the gospels at this date. Their central purpose and message are clear: they present God's saving plan for mankind.

Jesus speaks to us in and through his passion. We should endeavor to learn more about the Savior as we follow him during the last hours of his earthly life. After a brief word about the chronological setting of Jesus' life, and another about the predictions of the passion, we shall sit in on the Last Supper and observe the institution of the Eucharist. There too we shall listen once again to the marvellous farewell discourses of Jesus (Jn 13-17) which form a fitting preface to the actual passion account.

Chronological Setting

The gospels give more detail to the last days of Jesus' life than to any other portion of his life. All four evangelists describe the events of the last week at length.

We sometimes tend unconsciously to look upon Jesus Christ only as true God, and not as true Man. It requires an effort to consider him as someone who occupied a definite place in space and time. By way of introduction, then, we shall look into the question of his "time," to try to determine precisely *when* the great act of redemption took place. In order to do this, we must examine several texts:

Luke 3:1 The Beginning of the Public Ministry

From a chronological point of view this text of Luke is not very helpful. We know that Pilate held office for ten years (A.D. 26–36), Caiaphas for eighteen (A.D. 18–36), and Herod Philip from B.C. 4 to A.D. 34. These three sets of dates provide the boundaries *within which* Christ began his public career, but they do not pinpoint the date. Nor does "the fifteenth year of Tiberius Caesar" contribute the desired precision. This could be calculated from A.D. 12, when he may have been declared Augustus' colleague on the throne (no coins bear this out, all having either Augustus or Tiberius upon them), or from A.D. 14, when he actually became emperor. The fifteenth year from A.D. 12 is A.D. 26; from A.D. 14 it is A.D. 28, the first being too early, the second too late. Tiberius took office on August 19, A.D. 14, which means that the first Passover in Christ's public life would have been in A.D. 29, and if this were true, his public life would have to be limited to a single year, because he died in the year 30. A Syriac computation of this fifteenth year of Tiberius, however, yields October 1, A.D. 27 to September A.D. 28, as the fifteenth year. Since Luke was a native of Syrian Antioch, there is some plausibility to this view.

Luke 3:23 Jesus' Age During His Ministry

Christ was "about thirty years old" at the start of his public ministry, but we know little as to the date of that ministry. We know only that he was born sometime before the death of Herod the Great (B.C. 4). The imprecision of date concerning his birth is matched by the vague reference to his age at his death.

John 2:20 Herod's Temple

Josephus relates that Herod began to rebuild the Temple at Jerusalem in the eighteenth year of his reign, or B.C. 20–B.C. 10. From this date, forty-six years would yield A.D. 27/28 (cf. Ricciotti, *History* 11, 337ff).

John 8:57 Jesus' Age At His Death

Using this text, Irenaeus concluded that Christ was almost fifty years of age when he died. But in context, "fifty" was spoken in derision. Abraham saw his day? Abraham lived centuries before him (ca. B.C. 1800)! Even granting, for the sake of argument, that Christ was fifty years, half a century old, he could not possibly have seen Abraham! What they did not grasp was that Jesus was claiming pre-existence.

In conclusion, the chronological clues given in the New Testament texts do not give us certainty as to the exact beginning of Christ's public life.

A wide diversity of opinion likewise prevails concerning the length of Christ's public ministry, the various opinions reflecting both extremes, and many shades within the extremes. One author has felt that Mark's Gospel could be fitted into four-and-one-half months, Matthew's into five, and Luke's into six, and various Fathers of the Church held that the public ministry lasted for one, two, or three years.

A reading of the Synoptic Gospels leaves a definite impression that Christ had spent almost his entire public life in Galilee, making only one trip—the last—to Jerusalem. And yet John pictures a Christ who was almost always in Jerusalem. What is certain is that Christ spent his public ministry in much going and coming, and that he visited Jerusalem more than once. Proof seems contained in Mt 21:1–2; Mt 23:37; and Mt 26:17–19.

John's Gospel makes it almost certain that the public ministry of Jesus lasted for a fraction more than two years. John mentions three Passovers: the first in Jn 2:13, 23; the second in Jn 6:4; and the third in Jn 11:55; Jn 12:1; Jn 13:1. John also mentions Jesus' coming to Jerusalem on the occasion of a feast (5:1) but this can hardly be another Passover.

Predictions of the Passion

When in 27 or 28 A.D. Jesus began his public ministry, he preached a simple message: "Repent, for the kingdom of heaven is at hand." In the synagogue at Nazareth he startled everyone by declaring that Isaiah's words (61:1–2) referred to himself: "The spirit of the Lord is upon me . . . he has anointed me. He has sent me to bring glad tidings to the poor, to proclaim liberty to captives . . . to announce a year of favor from the Lord" (Lk 4:18–21). He began to perform cures of the sick, even on the sabbath, and as a teacher he manifested great independence of spirit, setting himself up as an interpreter of, and even greater than, the great lawgiver Moses.

Jesus' ministry soon drew the attention of the religious leaders of the nation. They challenged his authority, but he was not intimidated. He was, in fact, more than a match for them, and soon their public discomfort turned into active resentment. The sight of so many people flocking after him added fuel to the fire. But crowds, even when they follow you, are bad, as Camus observed. Those that followed Jesus soon lost interest in him; his picture of a meek and humble Messiah held little promise for men on the lookout for a strong national leader. Jesus was quite aware of this turn of events, and his teaching changed. Instead of speaking plainly and with authority, as before, he began to teach in parabolic form. Parables are subtle stories. Their implications strike the hearer unexpectedly, forcing upon him the realization that he is being challenged in depth, and made to face issues he might prefer to avoid. At the same time, Jesus began to draw his disciples about him, and spent more and more time with them, preparing them for what was to come. There was not much time. The message was so new that they found it hard to grasp, at least until after Jesus' death and resurrection.

The tension building between Jesus and the authorities was plain enough. Sides were being chosen, and the situation promised inevitable violence. Prophets had been slain before him, and the austere John the Baptist had been put to death by a petty king to satisfy the hatred of a vindictive woman. Not surprisingly, then, Jesus one day informed his followers that "he must go to Jerusalem and suffer many things from the elders and chief priests and scribes, and be killed, and on the third day be raised" (Mt 16:21).

This was the first of three predictions concerning his coming passion, and a lesson in the cost of Messiahship. It was a difficult lesson. Peter, true to form, reacted against it, and sought to talk sense into his master. What he received for his pains was a stinging rebuke. "Get behind me, Satan! You are a hindrance to me; for you are not on the side of God, but of men" (v. 23).

Some time after this, Peter and James and John were privileged witnesses to Jesus' transfiguration (Mt 17:1–8). They saw and heard Jesus talking with Moses and Elijah about his coming death (see Lk 9:21), and heard a voice from the cloud signifying God's approval of him. Peter showed his impetuous nature by suggesting that he set up booths—the thrilling moment might thus be prolonged. But the next moment they were alone with Jesus. Some time after descending the mountain, Jesus made it clear that he was to suffer and die. This is the second prediction of the passion: "The Son of Man is to be delivered into the hands of men, and they will kill him, and he will be raised on the third day" (Mt 17:22–23).

The second prediction is clearer than the first. Jesus already knew that he was going to be betrayed into the hands of men. Men knew little about forgiveness. They would not forgive him, nor would Judas, until it was too late.

As much as a year may have passed before Jesus again

brought up the matter of his passion. As he and his disciples were preparing to set out for the Holy City for the Passover, he said: "Behold, we are going up to Jerusalem; and the Son of Man will be delivered to the chief priests and scribes, and they will condemn him to death, and deliver him to the Gentiles to be mocked and scourged and crucified, and he will be raised on the third day" (Mt 20:18–19).

These plain, unadorned words give no clue as to Jesus' inner feelings, but they were definitely unsettling. The Son of Man would not only be betrayed and sentenced to death, but subjected to torture and death. The disciples already have begun to taste fear, and would not desert him—yet. Jesus walked resolutely on ahead of them, like a shepherd leading his timorous sheep.

It is unlikely that these three predictions of Jesus' death were written after the fact; in their progressive clarity they may very well correspond to reality. Forgers are careful people, and would hardly have invented anything that would have shown the apostles up in so bad a light. They were not only uncomprehending, but their behavior was less than heroic. The gospels make it perfectly clear that they were just not prepared for Jesus' passion. They were also unprepared for his resurrection.

The Last Supper

The last meal that Jesus ate with the Twelve was a Passover meal. The Passover was a commemorative feast, recalling the meal eaten by the Israelites in Egypt on the night the angel of God struck down all the first-born of Egypt, forcing Pharaoh to allow the Chosen People to escape from a land of bondage (Ex 12:29ff). By the time of Christ, the feast of "deliverance" or Passover had become the most important feast of the entire year. The details of the meal were carefully prescribed. With the help of the Bible (Ex 12:2ff) and other Jewish writings such as the rabbinical *Pesachim*, compiled toward the mid-second century, it is possible to reconstruct a typical Passover meal.

The key text describing the Passover meal is found in Exodus:

They shall eat its roasted flesh that same night, with unleavened bread and bitter herbs. . . . This is how you are to eat it: with your loins girt, sandals on your feet, and your staff in hand, you shall eat like those who are in flight. It is the Passover of the Lord. (Ex 12:8, 11)

The Passover (or Paschal) supper began with a blessing of the feast and of the wine; the people present drank the first of four cups of wine. Each man had his own cup. When all had washed their right hands, the first course began. It was a sort of hors d'oeuvres: bitter herbs (endive, chicory, wild lettuce—not garden vegetables but desert plants) well-seasoned with *haroseth*, a sauce made of pounded nuts, fruit, and vinegar (modern Jews use horseradish). This was eaten in memory of the bitter days in Egypt.

Next the roasted Paschal lamb was brought in, and the head of the house, at the request of his son, explained the symbolism of the food. The unleavened bread or *matsah* (Ex 13:18), was a recollection of the bread eaten in Egypt in haste (not waiting for the dough to rise). The lamb recalled the blood smeared on their doorposts to divert the avenging angel (Ex 12:23). The wine symbolized the joy and gratitude due to God for his benefactions. This was followed by the first part of the Hallel or songs of praise (Ps 112–113:8) and the second cup of wine was then drunk.

All present next washed both hands, and the main course was begun. The father of the house first blessed, broke, and distributed the unleavened bread, and then the lamb was eaten along with bitter herbs, and perhaps other foods like eggs and meats as well. After the lamb was eaten the third cup was poured out and an act of thanksgiving was made, the cup passing from one to another. This was the end of the meal. The lamb had to be completely eaten up and the supper finished by midnight (but Ex 12:10 seems to allow a longer time for this, perhaps until morning). Then the remainder of the Hallel (Ps 113:9 to 118) was sung, and the fourth cup of wine drunk.

The evangelists make no reference to the paschal lamb itself at the Last Supper, possibly because they attached little importance to the observance of a feast which, by this very meal, was being replaced by another, greater feast. Others have held that Jesus did not observe the Passover; the Last Supper was merely a Quiddush or rite of sanctification, observed before major feast days like Passover and involving two breads and a bottle of wine.

CHAPTER TWO

The Last Supper (John 13–17)

As Jesus came together with the apostles for their last meal, his ministry was approaching its culmination. At this point, the Jews had steadfastly rejected Jesus' appeals, but despite that he would carry on his work. His passion and death, prophecies soon to be realized, lay ahead, and would be followed by his resurrection and ascension. Before any of these things happened, he made a point of showing the disciples just how much he loved them, in a scene acted out against the background of the Passover meal. John wrote after the other evangelists, and seems to have taken for granted that everyone knew how the apostles came to be in that particular room. Instead John concentrated on what Jesus said and did at the Last Supper.

The chronology of the first part of the meal is taken mainly from chapter 13 of John. One insert comes from Luke.

1. The Washing of the Feet (13:1–11)
2. Explanation of the Washing (12–20)
3. Judas' Departure (21–30)
4. Institution of the Eucharist (Lk 22:20)
5. Discourse on Departure (31–38)

The Washing of the Feet (13:1–11)

The reader finds himself abruptly transferred to an Upper Room where a scene of great significance was about to take place. According to Luke (22:24), the apostles were engaged in an argument about reputation and precedence, and Jesus chose that moment to perform a symbolic act that would give his followers an unforgettable lesson in humility and fraternal charity. He washed their feet.

Before the feast of the Passover, which was the following day, Jesus realized that his hour had come; he was soon to die and return to the Father. This was the moment he chose to give his disciples an astonishing proof of his love. He would show his love for them to the end—that is, not to the end of his life, but to the ultimate degree of love.

During the supper, Judas' diabolical resolve to betray his Master, standing out in stark contrast to the Master's love, heightened the pathos of the hour (Jn 1:11), and emphasized the immensity of Jesus' forbearance. Aware as he was of Judas' scheme of betrayal, Jesus gave a practical example of his own immense charity.

What precisely was this washing of the feet? In a land where sandals were the ordinary footwear, and travellers moved on dusty, muddy roads, hosts customarily provided water for bathing the feet as one entered the house (but cf Lk 8:44). The task was relegated to the slaves and servants of the household. Christ's unusual action occurred, however, half way through the supper.

Some of the Fathers have seen more in Christ's extraordinary behavior than humility and an example of service. Origen and St. Jerome, for example, thought it was a rite to prepare the apostles for preaching; St. Augustine thought it meant a cleansing away of venial sins in immediate preparation for the Eucharist; Maldonatus suggested that it was a symbol of penance which remits even grave faults. Chrysostom, however, and many modern commentators, interpret the washing of the Apostles' feet as an extraordinary example of great humility.

Knowing that all power rested in his hands, Jesus arose from the couch where he was reclining, put aside his outer garment, took up a cloth and an ordinary basin and, like a servant (1 Sm 25:41) began to wash and dry the disciples' feet. The scene is highly dramatic. One can imagine the bewilderment of the disciples as they watched their Master thus abase himself. Jesus was not unaware of the impact of his actions; his knowledge of what Judas was about to do added special meaning to them.

Although Peter's primacy imposed no obligations upon the Master, it is natural to suppose that he washed that apostle's feet first of all. (Chrysostom thought he began with Judas.) Peter was quick to react to the spectacle of the Master at his feet. He drew back, and his inner turmoil found expression in the almost incoherent: "Lord! you washing my feet?" Since Peter had not grasped the fact that Jesus' ultimate humiliation was to be the effective cause of man's salvation, he found it difficult to understand Jesus' self-humiliation, and was upset that he should be the object of such an action. The contest here was not so much between Peter's pride and Jesus' humility as between ignorance and knowledge. Jesus said gently, What I do you do not understand (v. 7); allow me to continue. Peter, unable to grasp this, exploded with the emphatic: "You'll not wash my feet, ever!" Nowhere else does John, in recording Peter's vigorous reaction and Jesus' serene reply, sound so much like Mark.

Jesus then quietly said to Peter, "Either you let me do as I see fit, or you will have no part with me." There is no place in the Kingdom for those who will not accept the Master's way of doing things. Peter quite typically went to the other extreme and insisted that Christ wash "not only my feet, but my hands and my head as well." The last thing he wanted was to be separated from Christ, but at the same time, he could not resist telling the Master what he should do. It was not the first time Peter gave evidence of self-will (cf Mt 16:22).

At another time Jesus might have smiled patiently at Peter, but not now. "The man who has bathed has no need to wash: he is entirely cleansed." In other words, this washing was not a mere purification or cleansing, but an example of service and humility. And it was example given under trying circumstances, for Jesus knew that the traitor was soon to betray him.

Indeed, after assuring Peter that he had no need of a complete bath, Jesus remarked with some sadness, "You are clean, but not all." He had known from the beginning that one of the Twelve would betray him (6:71); only now did he refer to it for the first time. With customary tact and exquisite charity, he did not openly denounce his betrayer. But Judas, immune to such delicacy, made no move to prevent the Master from washing his feet.

The Explanation (*Jn 13:12–20*)

Jesus had given the apostles a lesson that domineering authority and humility are not compatible. He wanted these future leaders to be humbly charitable toward others, even to their subjects. If *he* could stoop to wash their feet without losing his dignity, *they* could humble themselves without losing theirs. The lesson was easy to grasp, and of value if put into practice, but not all would put it into practice well. Once you know all these things, blessed will you be if you put them into practice. Blessedness depends not on knowledge of the truth but upon *doing* the truth. The theme of mutual love, which is the very heart and soul of the Church, is thus introduced.

Jesus had known that one of the men he had chosen would betray him, but he had chosen Judas so that the scripture might be fulfilled. He did not exclude Judas from his charity; Judas did that himself. Jesus quotes Psalm 41:9 "He who ate of my bread, has lifted his heel against me." The reference is to David, a figure of the Messiah. David was basely betrayed by his trusted counselor Achitophel during Absalom's conspiracy (2 Sm 15–16). To eat bread at the table of a superior was by its nature a profession of loyalty and friendship; *to lift the heel* is a graphic image of the explosive violence of an animal's kick. Men too can act in a brute fashion.

Jesus thus clearly announces at this time that one of the Twelve would betray him. It was important that he anticipate the Apostles' disappointment and discouragement. What might seem to men to be complete failure was part of a divine plan. They could trust absolutely in him who had foreseen not only the main event, but also the details.

"I tell you now, before it takes place so that later on you

may believe that I am." A certain obscurity hovers over Jesus' words. If the phrase "that I am" is taken as it stands, and "I AM" is the very name of God (Ex 4:14), the words are Christ's claim to share in the transcendence of God; or they can mean the Messiah or Master—the omniscient Son of God. The latter is the most probable meaning.

Jesus had reminded the disciples that their dignity was not greater than his, but it was very great just the same. Those who receive the apostles with honor will also receive Christ, and those who receive Christ receive also the Father who sent him.

The Church has never considered the Washing of the Feet as one of the sacraments. She has simply judged, as she has a right to do, that Christ's command that we are to wash each other's feet was not to be taken literally, but is to be understood as a lesson whose spirit should be faithfully retained (1 Tm 5:10). The Master's action in washing his apostles' feet is a powerful example of true humility and love.

Hoskyns remarks that the liturgical washing of the feet is more than a mere commemoration of an isolated incident in Christ's life, and more than an exhortation to humility. "It forms part of the thought of the incarnation, the Death, and the Resurrection of the Son of God. This is what lies behind the peculiar significance that was attached to the removal and taking up again of the vestments. For Christian humility is dependent upon the humiliation and the glorification of Christ."

The washing of the feet is often done on Holy Thursday, but it has never been made obligatory on all Christians. Christian kings and queens used to wash the feet of twelve poor men on Maundy Thursday as a sign of humility.

The Departure of Judas (13:21–30)

Judas was present at the supper, but Jesus' words found no echo in his heart. However, Christ was troubled by the presence of the traitor, and, all at once overwhelmed by sadness, seemed suddenly to find Judas' presence almost too much. Slowly but distinctly, he said, "I tell you solemnly one of you will betray me." No obscure hint now, as in vv. 10–11; one of the Twelve was being singled out. Christ's words were as lightning splitting the darkness. Consternation must have seized the disciples in the silence that followed. So well had Judas hidden his hand that only Jesus, with his supernatural knowledge, knew of his plan of betrayal. Leonardo da Vinci has immortalized this startling moment in his painting of the Last Supper.

The guests reclined on carpets or mattresses, lying on their left side, supported by the left elbow. They lay obliquely around the food, so that the head of one guest would be level with the breast of the person on his left. It is not likely that the apostles, who often ate their meals sitting on the ground or walking along the roads, always kept the same place, but on this occasion it would seem that John was next to Jesus and Peter farther off, so that he could not directly speak to the Master. Presuming that John either knew the answer or could easily find out, Peter signaled to him to ask Jesus whom he meant. The beloved disciple leaned back until his head rested upon Jesus' bosom and asked quietly, "Who is he, Lord?" So unassailable is the purity of Christ that John does not hesitate to describe, with the accuracy of an interested eyewitness, exactly how this exchange of whispers took place.

Jesus answered the question, but only for the benefit of Peter and John who had asked it. We do not know how, or even if, John relayed the answer to Peter; perhaps a sign sufficed. The answer was, "the one to whom I give the bit of food I dip in the dish." It was customary for the host to dip a choice morsel from the central bowl, using bread instead of a fork, and hand it to a guest, and Jesus may have done this rapidly to several of the disciples in succession, so that John was not able to clearly identify the traitor.

Jesus' conciliatory gesture was an appeal to Judas' better nature. It met with no response. Judas no longer felt himself one with the disciples, or with Christ. He had severed relations with them and no longer belonged with them at table. Jesus said to him, "Do it quickly. Don't waste any time now." Obviously not a command to do evil, these words were rather the last words of a discouraged friend.

At the time, none of the disciples except Judas understood the meaning of Jesus' command. Since Judas had handled the group's money, they may have thought that he was to buy something that was lacking for the feast (the "legal" feast was the following day), or perhaps that he was to give alms which would enable some poor family to celebrate the feast properly on the morrow.

Judas went out, after having eaten the morsel Christ offered him. In accepting this, he violated the basic rule which binds those who eat together, and apparently he did so callously, to avoid attracting attention to himself. He was undoubtedly relieved to have gotten out of the room safely. John says of this moment, "it was night," an intensely dramatic statement evoking the whole symbolism of light and darkness. Now was the hour of darkness, the hour of those dark and unseen powers which were enthroned in the troubled soul of Judas. But it was also the hour for the most intimate discourses of our Lord; now as never before, the light shone in the darkness.

Did Judas receive the Eucharist at the Last Supper? Probably not, for it would seem that the Eucharist was instituted after the announcement of the betrayal, as Matthew and Mark have it. Luke's order seems less preferable here. John makes no mention of the institution of the Eucharist, simply noting that Judas went out but not saying when that occurred.

The Institution of the Eucharist (Lk 22:20)

At the end of the Passover meal (Lk 22:20), Jesus took bread, gave thanks, broke it, and gave it to the disciples. He no doubt used unleavened bread, since this was prescribed for the feast; the term *artos* used here usually means leavened bread. Only Matthew and Mark say that Christ blessed the bread; Luke and Paul, that he gave thanks. There was a tradition that his blessing of the bread and wine was one of thanksgiving, hence the name Eucharist (thanksgiving) given to this sacrament.

Jesus said, "This is my body which will be given up for you." The subject of the sentence (this) does not refer to Christ but to the bread he held in his hands; the verb *is* (in the Greek but not in Aramaic) expresses the identity of subject and predicate. Jesus clearly states that the bread becomes and is his body, not that his body is *in* or *with* the bread. A "transubstantiation," as we call it, has taken place, only the accidents of the bread and the wine remaining—without a subject! Something wholly unexpected, unsuspected by Aristotle. Luke and Paul add "which will be given for you," indicating thus the sacrificial character of this new rite; the "for you" signifies that it has satisfactory value as well.

"Do this as a memorial of me," Jesus continued. The Council of Trent has defined these words to mean that Christ thus ordained his disciples priests, for the sacrifice instituted by his words requires those who can perform the sacrifice over and over again. What they shall do constitutes a memorial rite, not merely a symbolic one like the Paschal lamb which was really immolated and eaten, but in commemoration of a real deliverance. In repeating Christ's words and actions, the disciples will bring about the same effect: the conversion of the bread and wine into Jesus' body and blood.

"This is the cup of my blood, of the new and eternal covenant, which is to be poured out for you and for many for the forgiveness of sins." "This"—namely, the wine in the cup I hold in my hands—is my blood of the new alliance (testament), sealed, as alliances are, with blood, my blood (see Ex 24:8). It is the "testament," the will of Christ who is about to die and who makes disposition of his blood.

"Poured out" is a present participle, that is, "it is being poured out." The present tense indicates that the shedding of Jesus' blood on Calvary is reproduced in a mystical way by the new rite. From this moment the effusion of Christ's blood is envisaged as a sacrifice.

"For many." The universality of salvation is expressed by these words which mark the contrast between the "one" who dies and the "many" who will profit from his death. Christ died for all men; but not all will profit from this. *Pollon* or "many" stands for the community. No one is excluded. The new liturgy makes this explicit. The blood of the new and everlasting covenant "will be shed for . . . all men."

Prelude to the Last Discourse (Jn 13:31–38)

It has been remarked that the discourse of Jesus in the Upper Room, both sublime and deeply moving, is to John's Gospel what the Sermon on the Mount is to Matthew's. But do we have here the very words, the *ipsissima verba* of Christ? For many other discourses of Christ one reasonably supposes some alteration of form as the words passed through the successive filters of memory and faith. But it is also reasonable to suppose that the words spoken in the intimacy of the Upper Room on the eve of his death must have especially impressed themselves upon the minds of the apostles, and that even after a long lifetime John still remembered them well. These discourses approach as close to the words actually spoken by Jesus as the memory of one who heard them can bring us. Present here is one greater than the evangelist.

Judas' departure from the room cleared the air. His departure removed his oppressive presence and initiated, so to speak, the work of salvation; Jesus could now speak freely, tenderly, and intimately to those whom he affectionately called his little children. He did so with remarkable calm, for Judas' going was the beginning of the end.

By not avoiding the treachery of Judas, Christ resolutely set his foot upon the road leading to Calvary. He did so with such assurance and with so clear a vision of the end results that from this very moment he considered the outcome already certain. He said, "now is the Son of Man glorified, and God is glorified in him" (Jn 13:31). Too much emphasis should not be put on the word "now." As a man Christ had already been "glorified" (see 2:11; 11:4, 40; 12:23), but this glory would be heightened (12:23) because he labored to make the Father known (8:38) and glorified (7:18). Jesus sees the triumph ahead, and the first movement of the passion somehow encapsulates the glory awaiting him. Everything, in the end, will redound to God's glory, and his own.

Glory is the honor that is due to genuine excellence, a splendor visible to and recognized by many. God was honored in that his divine justice and love and mercy were admirably brought out by Jesus' death. Since God is glorified in Jesus, God will glorify Christ in himself. He will either take him up unto himself and thus manifest his own divinity and glory, or the divinity and glory of Jesus. The second explanation is preferable. Jesus could not renounce the glory proper to him as Son of God, but where his humanity was involved he could renounce the rights and privileges which were properly due to the Incarnate Word. He thus appeared as a man, like unto other men in all save sin. He hungered and thirsted, knew fatigue and disappointment, suffered and died. And it was because of his obedience that God exalted him, giving him the name that is above every other name, LORD (Phil 2:5–11).

Jesus' entry into glory was not possible while he remained with his disciples, so when he spoke to them of his departure it was in words of tenderness; they were his little children. What is surprising is that the words here, "where I go you shall not come," are the same as those he had once addressed to the Jews (7:34; 8:21). This did not escape Peter's attention; he now seems to be waiting his chance to say something. "Where I go you cannot come" can mean many things, depending upon the speaker's tone of voice or inflection or intention. Jesus' departure was no haphazard affair, but a deliberate inauguration of the way his little children must live, that is, without his visible presence. Without him they will have to lead a life of faith. However, the separation would be brief, because he will return and seek them out, and they will rejoin him in glory (14:2–3); it will be a definitive separation only for Christ's enemies.

At the moment of death, men often utter profound thoughts by which they are forever after remembered, and this is what Jesus now proceeds to do. "I give you a new commandment, Love one another . . . as I have loved you." The spirit of his love must pervade the community he has established; he makes this a law. "Maundy" Thursday derives from the Latin *mandatum novum* or "new commandment."

The disciples are then to love one another, not as men do, but as Christ has loved them (Rom 8:37). It is the mode and the extent of loving that is new, not the commandment itself (cf. Lv 19:18). Gone forever all snobbishness, clannishness, and mutual self-interest; this love will be illuminated by the Incarnation and warmed by the very sentiments of Christ (Jn 3:16). It calls for and obtains help from on high; Christ multiplies his graces to create in his followers a new heart (cf. Ez 36:26), the very heart of Christ (Phil 1:8).

Christ's new commandment has not always been faithfully carried out except by his spouse, the Church. This love has not been confined within a tight little circle of mutual admirers, but has overflowed upon the whole world. It is by the Church's works of charity that she still wins those souls who perceive that her works are motivated by her love for Christ. That love is a precious legacy from the Master.

Peter's Denial Foretold (13:38)

Peter, half-listening to what Christ was saying, finally opened his mouth, and promptly put his foot into it. "Lord, where do you mean to go?" Appreciating Peter's eagerness to serve him, Christ gently repeated his words, adding that Peter would indeed follow him, but later. It was a prophecy of Peter's martyrdom, but so veiled that Peter did not understand it. Instead, he misunderstood the Master's words. He seems to have thought that the Master would somehow slip away from them, or that their courage and his own had been brought into question, so he asked brusquely: "Why can I not follow you now? I will lay down my life for you."

Peter was to play an important part in the Church after Jesus' death, and would one day die for him. Now, however, Christ gently, reproachfully and somewhat ironically even repeated the words Peter had just uttered and declared that this brave disciple would three times disown him before the cock next crowed. So much for his brave words.

John 14: The Discourse After Supper

Jesus' luminous words at the Last Supper cast a mysterious spell over all who read them. The imminence of the Master's departure is in the air, and his words were designed to stir up the faith and hope and love of the apostles. He promises to help them by his renewed presence, and by the Paraclete the Father will send his request.

Chapter 14 can be divided as follows:

1. The "mansions" or dwelling places   vv. 1–3
2. The Way to the Father   vv. 4–11
3. The "Greater Works"   vv. 12–14
4. Promise of the Paraclete   vv. 15–17
5. The Manifestation of Christ   vv. 18–24
6. New Promise of the Holy Spirit   vv. 25–31

The "Mansions" (14:1–3)

The prediction of Peter's denial, following so closely upon the announcement of betrayal by one of his own, caused sadness in the disciples. Jesus knew by his own experience what inner distress was (11:33; 12:27; 13:21). He knew full well how deeply grieved they would be when left to fend for themselves, without his visible presence and strength to buoy them up. To soften the blow, then, he devoted his last hours to words of comfort, and as he spoke an atmosphere of calm descended upon the disciples.

"Do not let your hearts be troubled." The verb used for trouble (*tarraso*) may also describe a wind-tossed sea (Is 24:14; 51:15); the human heart, which in biblical language is the seat of both feeling and faith (Rom 10:10), can be tossed about by sudden storms of grief and fear, but the apostles must be stout of heart. You believe in God; with that same kind of faith, believe in me. Without faith in his divinity they will view his going from them as pure disaster; if, however, they believe in him, all will be well. He promises to return to visit them, bringing with him the Father and the Holy Spirit.

The famous temple of Jerusalem was built by Solomon (2 Chr 3–4), rebuilt and enlarged by Herod the Great, and contained many chambers. We do not know the dimensions of the Upper Room of the Last Supper, but it foreshadowed something larger and better. Jesus tells his loved ones, "In my Father's house there are many mansions." The term *mone* or "mansions" signifies a lodging, or halting-place. Heaven, like a spacious palace, will be able to accommodate an indefinite number of guests; there will be plenty of room for everybody. The main idea is that God will not dwell alone, in solitary splendor, surrounded only by angels; the door is open to those who loved him on earth. It is improbable that *mone* should be taken to mean stages in a journey, as if in heaven one will progress from one reward to another. Nor is there anything in the context to suggest differing degrees of glory, however obvious it is that not all will be "housed" in heaven with equal dignity.

If there was to be no room for the disciples in his Father's house, Jesus would not have been so cruel as to raise in them the hope of rejoining him there (see 12:26). He deliberately raises that hope: "otherwise how could I have told you that I am going to prepare a place for you?" The mansions or chambers are there, and he goes on ahead to prepare them. He is the forerunner; he will take possession of the rooms for them (Heb 6:20). For the present, their part in the affair will consist in being prepared by him, and this he will do by sending the Holy Spirit upon them, applying to them the fruits of his passion, and drawing their hearts to him. With his usual flair St. Augustine writes, "He prepares the dwellings by preparing the dwellers."

How comforting it must have been for the apostles to hear that they would not only be admitted into the Father's house, but then would also be there with their beloved Master. "I shall come back to take you with me; that where I am you also may be." When was Jesus to return? The words are hardly a reference to his final coming in glory. Do they refer to the invisible return of Christ by grace, or to the moment of death of each Christian believer? The words rather reflect a comparison that is consistently carried through. Jesus goes ahead to prepare for them, and he will return to tell them that all is ready. The faithful servant will not be separated from his Master. From the earliest days to the end of time, the Church awaits with confidence the fulfillment of this promise. *Maranatha*, "Lord, Come!"

The Way to the Father (14:4–11)

Jesus had repeatedly stated that he was going to his Father, but the disciples failed to grasp his meaning (see 13:36). But now they could understand this. "(To go) where I go, you know the way." When he returns, it is important that he find them on the right road, ready for him. The road is the road of charity (13:34).

The disciples were not enlightened by Jesus' statement, but only more perplexed. Thomas was unwilling to proceed on such a basis, and plainly declared: "Lord, we do not know where you are going; how can we know the way." Jesus might very well be going to the Father. What true Israelite was not? What road does Jesus have in mind? What was its destination? The Master had earlier refused to give Peter a direct answer to the question of where he was going (13:36); how can he now say that they also know the way? It was confusing. Thomas' perplexity, not too respectful, was understandable, and it was to lead to an astounding development of Jesus' enigmatic words. Jesus revealed that he was not only the forerunner, but is in fact the way itself and the truth and the life. "Way" has a moral and religious meaning.

No prophet or teacher of old ever dared identify himself with the way of the Lord (Dt 5:32–33; Is 30:11; Ps 16:11). Jesus makes his claim quietly but unequivocally. He is not a method or law, no mere guide or model, but the door to God (10:7–9)—the way itself. He is the only bridge between God and man. No one can reach the end of the way which is God except through faith in him. "No one comes to the Father but through me." Whoever does follow Jesus reaches the desired goal.

Jesus had often spoken about truth. Now he declares that he himself is not distinct from it, as a legislator is distinct from the law he frames, or a teacher from the subject matter he expounds. Jesus identifies himself with truth. He *is* its personal and substantial embodiment, the perfect expression of God's revelation and of God himself. He who believes in Jesus needs no further knowledge; not only is he sure of reaching the goal, but he has in a sense already laid hold of it, for in Jesus, truth and way are complementary terms. The Christian life is walking in the way of truth (4:23).

Jesus is also the life. He is his being, substantially and personally living, and the source of all other life. (John uses the word "life" thirty-seven times in his gospel.) His life was the light of men (1:4); he came that they might have life and have it to the full. "I am the resurrection and the life" (10:10; 11:25). He is food and drink, and his words are words of eternal life (6:68). Apart from him there is no life, only death. This is eternal life, to know the Father present in the Son (17:3).

The unqualified way in which Jesus identifies himself as truth and life suggests that he is not only the way leading to God, but that he is God himself, of the same nature as the Father whose revelation he is (17:3). "If you really know me, you would know my father also" (14:7). This "if" stands for a "since" or "because," and the words are both consolation and promise. Under the circumstances, it is unlikely that Jesus was rebuking or excusing the disciples. In knowing Jesus, the apostles both know the Father and have seen him.

Philip spoke up, "Lord, show us the Father and that will be enough for us." No one blames Philip for his bewilderment. All Jews knew of the grandiose visions of God which had been granted to Moses and the Prophet Isaiah. Philip was asking that he be allowed to see the Father through a similar bodily vision. Not to be overlooked is Philip's confidence that Jesus could manage even that.

Jesus' reply was quite unexpected and again not wholly clear. Your request has already been answered, Philip. "Whoever has seen me has seen the Father." Philip must learn to be content with faith. The Incarnate Word is the only revelation of the Father he will have for now; to recognize Christ's divinity is to recognize the Father, for Father and Son are one. Such a seeing is not a material vision, but something spiritual. He who sees Jesus sees the Father.

What followed next was a stunning revelation concerning the inner, personal life of God. "Do you not believe that I am in the Father and the Father is in me?" In one breath Jesus affirms that he is God; in the next he distinguishes himself from the Father; one in nature, they are two different persons. Jesus is the Son; he is also man. Because of the mutual immanence of Father and Son (also called *circuminsession*), where the one is, the other is also. The words that Jesus speaks he does not speak as man; he has direct knowledge of God and of his will (7:16; 8:28; 12:49). It is Jesus who speaks and acts, but it is the Father acting. "The words I speak are not spoken of myself, it is the Father who lives in me accomplishing his works." There is no appeal here to the sublimity of Jesus' doctrine, nor any argument based on the miraculous character of his works, but rather Jesus' testimony in a matter he alone can speak of, namely, that the Father is the divine principle of his words and works.

On anybody else's lips words like these would have been blasphemy. Yet Jesus calmly asks the apostles to accept the fact: "I am in the Father and the Father is in me." God was in the prophets, but nowhere was it ever suggested that they were in him, as Jesus claims to be. If the apostles will not believe on his word alone, they have only to consider the significance of his miracles. "Believe because of the works I do." God would not have given such striking approval to a liar and a blasphemer.

The Greater Works (14:12–14)

Miracles have not ceased with the death of Christ the Miracle-Worker. In fact, so intimate is the union set up by faith between the believer and Christ that the believer can perform the same miracles as his Master. During Jesus' life the apostles received power to do as he did (Mk 6:7, 13; Mt 10:8), and they actually performed physical cures. Not all of Jesus' works, however, were miraculous. His outstanding characteristic was his acceptance of God's will, and his self-sacrifice. In this the apostles could and would imitate him well. But he says something else here—they shall do greater works than he did, because he is going to the Father (v. 12).

It is impossible to imagine the apostles performing miracles greater than the raising of Lazarus, the feeding of the five thousand with a few loaves and fishes, the stilling of the tempest on the sea of Galilee, or the turning of water into wine. It is not precisely in the continuance of such astonishing miracles that Christ's promise is fulfilled. Jesus was speaking of his messianic work, and it is here that the apostles will do greater works than he. His earthly life had been limited by the circumstance of place and by his mission to the Chosen People, but once he entered into glory, such limitations of the messianic mission would cease, and the works of his disciples would surpass his (10:16–18; 11:52). Nevertheless, these greater works depend on Jesus' return to the Father.

The contrast Jesus is making here is between the few who preach and the many who shall be converted; between the mission of Jesus to the Jews, and that of the apostles of the world. Nothing in the record of Jesus' ministry can compare with the conversion and baptism of 3,000 on Pentecost, and nothing in that ministry can compare with Paul's planting the Church in four great provinces of the Empire. These greater works are possible "because I go to the Father" (v. 12). The greater power granted to the apostles comes through Christ our Lord.

Prayer to God is as old as mankind. The disciples already know how to pray to the Father. Now that they are to do Jesus' work, Jesus tells them that they should pray to the Father in his name. "Whatever you ask in my name I will do, so as to glorify the Father in the Son" (v. 13). *En to onomati mou*—"in my name"—appears here for the first time, but frequently hereafter. The apostles will begin at once to ask "in Jesus' name" (cf Acts 3:6,16; 4:10; 5:40; 16:18; Mk 16:17). This may mean that they will act and pray as belonging to him, or as authorized and empowered by him (cf 5:43; 10:25) to approach the Father. All must approach God in prayer, not as having in themselves any claim to be heard, but confident of their union with Jesus who is the beloved Son whom the Father hears and always answers (11:42).

"Anything you ask me in my name I will do" (v. 14). Prayers directed to Christ also will be heard, because offered by his servants and in accordance with his will (1 Jn 5:14–16). Such prayers must be consonant with "my name," that is, they must fit in with Jesus' saving purpose and be connected with the good of the Church. Everything about Christ—his Incarnation, death, resurrection and ascension—point to his unswerving purpose to lead mankind back to God.

Jesus Will Send the Paraclete (14:15–17)

To Jesus the future is an open book, and he speaks next of a necessary condition for the reception of the Holy Spirit: "If you love me, keep my commandments" (v. 15). Jesus, the first Paraclete (1 Jn 2:1), will ask the Father to send another Paraclete, another Defender, an Advocate or powerful friend. He will not be a mere force or power, but a distinct Person, "to be with you always" (v. 16) in a spiritual way. Jesus' historical presence in the world was brief; his spiritual presence "unto the consummation of the world" is fulfilled through the Spirit who is distinct from him but not of another nature or function.

The world desires only what it sees (see 1 Cor 2:14); it has no welcome for, and cannot receive, the invisible Spirit of Truth, the revealer and source of all true religion (4:23). Because it cannot see, the world will not know or possess him. As for the disciples, the presence of the Paraclete within them brings a knowledge which leads to a greater perception; they are brought into intimate contact with this Spirit. Even before Pentecost, the Spirit was stirring in their hearts. This foretaste of what lay ahead distinguished them from their unbelieving contemporaries. "You can recognize him because he remains with you and will be within you" (v. 17). Since God alone can "indwell" in another, the Spirit must be divine (see v. 23, 26).

The Manifestation of Christ to His Disciples (14:18–24)

The promise of another Defender was not exactly encouraging to the apostles inasmuch as it suggested that Jesus was leaving them. To leave them without the hope of seeing him again would have been to leave his "little children" orphans. He called them his children, and was like a father to them. He reassured them then that between his death and his glorious return at the end of time, "I will come back to you" (v. 18). This return is not the Parousia, his appearance at the end of time, nor his appearances to the disciples after the resurrection. His words refer to the invisible coming of Christ after the resurrection, a coming not limited to the short period he would remain on earth, but something extending throughout their lives. No one specific application of this phrase exhausts its meaning. Jesus does not come to his own unaccompanied, the Father and the Holy Spirit are always with him.

In a few more hours, the Incarnate Word would disappear from the world. "Yet a little while and the world will see me no more." But the disciples are not the world, and they shall see him "who has life, and you will have life" (v. 19). Risen from the dead, Jesus shall live his glorious life forever, and the apostles who remain under his spiritual influence shall live by and in him as branches in the vine (15:14). They shall, moreover, be conscious of living this new (but not wholly new) divine life.

When the disciples live a life of union with Christ, they will understand what they now find so difficult—that Jesus is one with his Father and of the same divine nature as he. "On that day you will know that I am in my Father, and you in me, and I in you" (v. 20). Nor is this all: with the mutual immanence of the Father and Son comes the reward which awaits faith and love, namely, a mutual co-existence between Jesus and the faithful who love him. "He who loves me will be loved by my Father, and I too will love him and reveal myself to him" (v. 21). They shall know by a kind of experience that God is in them by his grace, that Jesus Christ is living in them (Eph 3:17), and that he has not abandoned them.

Christ's return, like that of the Paraclete, depends upon the fulfillment of an important condition: one must love him and prove that love by keeping his commandments. "He who obeys the commandments he has from me is the man who loves me" (v. 21). The words seem to have been uttered with future generations of believers in mind. St. Augustine says, "We too learn, as if we were there 'with them.' " To know that one is loved is sweet, and awakens a greater love for the one who loves; in loving Jesus, the disciples arouse the Father's love for them. "He who loves me will be loved by my Father"

(v. 21). And not only does the love one bears the Son attract the benevolence of the Father; it arouses a greater love on the part of Christ as well, and he promises to manifest himself in a relatively clearer way: "I too will love him and reveal myself to him" (v. 21). This promise is fulfilled by the granting of graces, especially during times of prayer. Jesus gives himself to his beloved children as a source and motive power; acting through the sacraments, giving himself in the Eucharist and speaking through the mouths of his ministers. The light does not dispel all mystery; it leads to an ever-growing but veiled kind of understanding.

Jesus' promise to reveal himself to his disciples and not to the world prompted Judas (not the Iscariot but Thaddeus) to speak out. "Lord why is it that you will reveal yourself to us, and not to the world" (v. 22)? Judas could not understand how the Messiah could be hidden from the world in which he was to set up his glorious throne. Were there to be limits imposed on God's power? In reply Jesus repeated his teaching that his revelation of himself is reserved for those who love and keep his commandments: "Anyone who loves me, be true to my word and my Father will love him." The world cannot know because it does not love. Jesus goes on: "and we will come to him and make our dwelling place with him" (v. 23). The Trinity will reside in the souls of the just (vv. 17, 23, 27). The presence of the Trinity can be known only by loving knowledge, so the world which does not love is deprived of this manifestation of God.

Judas asked how Christ would reveal himself to the world, St. Augustine remarks, and is instructed instead about love and the indwelling. Jesus will manifest himself as he said he would, but, as he promised, this will be a manifestation only to those who love him.

CHAPTER THREE

Farewell Discourses

John 15: The Discourses at the Last Supper

John 14 ends with Jesus saying: "Rise, let us go hence." One then imagines the little group leaving the Upper Room and starting off for Gethsemani. But there then follow three chapters (15–17) which interrupt the sequence of 14:31 and 18:1, and continue the discourses in the Upper Room. Several interesting guesses have been made to explain this literary unevenness.

The first explanation rests upon a commonly observed phenomenon: dinner guests will frequently bid farewell to their host for the evening, and then stand at the door talking for some time. Did this happen in this case? Possibly, but probably not. John 15:1 to 16:15 contains the longest monologue in the entire gospel; a more logical place for it would have been at the table. A second suggestion is that Jesus uttered these words while the group made its way toward Gethsemani. However, given the steepness of the path and the hilly terrain, this is not very likely; one walks best single-file on hill sides. A third solution has been sought in a rearrangement of these chapters, thus:

1: John 12; then 15–17; then 13–14, *or*
2: John 13:1–31a; 15–16; 13–31b–14:31; 17, *or*
3: John 14:1–31; 16:4–33; 15:1–16:4; 17.

Much can be said for this suggestion. John, like Matthew, may have inserted here sayings of the Lord which had been uttered at different times. The historical unity of John 15–17 could be like that in the Sermon on the Mount (Mt 5–7), in Jesus' instruction to his Apostles (Mt 10:6–42), or in the "eschatological discourse" (Mt 24). Indeed, John 15:1–17 treats Jesus' union with his disciples without reference to his imminent departure. Chronologically the words in this section could fit in comfortably after his choice of the Twelve, and before he sent them forth to preach (cf. Mt 10). When read in the context of the Last Supper, the words become more significant, almost melancholic in tone. From a theological view, the Father in these verses is considered to be distinct from the Son, but nothing is explicitly said of the unity between Father and Son as in John 14.

In John 15:18–16:4, Jesus foresees the hatred of the world for his followers. These words match some of the ideas contained in the Synoptics' eschatological discourse (cf. Mt 24). The Father sends the Son, but—since nothing here suggests their sharing in the same divine nature—the words may reflect an earlier stage of Jesus' revelation of himself to his disciples.

John 16:4b–33 centers about the promise of the Holy Spirit, the assurance that Jesus will return, and the awakening of the disciples' faith in him. This section resembles chapter 14. The words fit easily into the discourse at the Last Supper, but with this difference—this section is a supplement to the other. It is probable that these were *not* among Jesus' last words, as they too seem to reflect an early stage of the instruction he gave to his disciples. The light is not complete.

This reconstruction validates John's reliability in historical matters, for even while these verses may be displaced and given a special nuance, they preserve their primitive meaning. Chapters 15 and 16 can be usefully divided in the following manner:

1. The Vine and the Branches (vv. 1–8)
2. Union with Jesus through Love (vv. 9–17)
3. Hatred of the World—Future Persecutions (vv. 18–16:4)

4. Jesus' Departure (vv. 16:4–33)
   a. Promise of the Holy Spirit (vv. 5–15)
   b. Jesus Will Return (vv. 16–23)
   c. Prayer is Always Heard (vv. 23–24)
   d. Faith in Christ (vv. 28–33)

The Vine and the Branches (15:1–8)

The teaching that Jesus is for his disciples what the vine is for its branches is applicable to all disciples. Here this illustration is given to the first group of disciples who shall go out as his apostles and bear fruit. Such a discourse would fit the occasion when Jesus had chosen the Twelve; placed here, it develops the theme of union: the results of the union between the Master and his disciples will be fruits of charity. This theme is not a farewell, but could be attached to a farewell since it contains an important truth which those who are to do the master's work must know. The pericope also fits in well with the Last Supper where the Eucharist has been celebrated with wine, and also because of the earlier allusion Jesus has made to the fruit of the vine.

Outlining the main purpose of the discourse, certain ideas and words crop up again and again: fruit, eight times; love, four times; prayer heard, twice; abide, in a mystical sense, eleven times. Having just given himself in the Eucharist, Jesus asks his disciples to abide in him so that he and his words abide in them. There is a special nuance, then, given this discourse in the charged atmosphere of the Last Supper, even if the image originally introduced a new and intimate relationship between the disciples and Jesus.

At various times Jesus made it plain that he was replacing certain Jewish institutions and feasts. Now he applies to himself the figure which was so often used in the Old Testament of Israel: "I am the true vine" (v. 1). In the Old Testament, references to Israel as the Lord's vine were not complimentary; as a vine, Israel had been a great disappointment (Is 5; Jer 2:21; Ez 15). But Jesus is the true vine—the vine worthy of the name.

Viniculture in Palestine is not as highly developed as elsewhere; for example, the vines do not hang on trellises but are barely off the ground. But the land abounds in vines and the image could come naturally to Jesus' mind. At the Last Supper he had said, "I will no more drink of the fruit of the vine" (Mt 26:29), and that may have led John to insert it here.

"My Father is the vinedresser." (All attempts to find hints here as to the relationship between Father and Son in the Trinity are misplaced.) Even God's vine needs careful attention; the vine cannot help itself. Vines are everywhere trimmed in the spring of the year. Branches which promise no fruit are cut off. Those that bear tiny grapes are carefully trimmed of the non-bearing shoots and twigs which would absorb the life-giving sap of the vine to no purpose. "Every branch in me that does not bear fruit he [the Father] will take away" (v. 2). Jesus, not Israel, is the vine and the disciples, not the Jews, are the branches. Fruit means good works, a holy life according to the commandments, especially that of love. For the disciples, fruit will mean bringing others to Christ. The disciple who is without faith or love will soon be cut off; one who believes and loves shall be regularly pruned. When this pruning shall be done is not said, but in the ordinary course of events, it is generally done by sufferings, even by death.

Jesus the true vine is not some impersonal being but the Incarnate Word, the Man-God, the principle of grace and Head of the Church. He unites all men in himself. Christ is not the vine of the heavenly Father independently of the branches on the vine. The vine and its branches are of the same nature, which means that Jesus' followers must be divinized by grace, form one body with him, and look to him who is the head for governing. This union is a corporate, vital, and effective one.

"You are pruned already by means of the word which I have spoken to you" (v. 3). The parable is interrupted here and Jesus speaks directly to his disciples. He has said they are already washed clean (13:10). They will grow further, but only through their union with the vine. The Father did not operate directly on the disciples to cleanse them, but the Son cleansed them through his word (cf. Rom 1:16; 1 Pt 1:23). There is contrast here. The pruning-knife and hook are extrinsic to the vine, but Jesus' word is an inward source of life, transforming and strengthening his disciples from within.

"Abide in me, and I in you" (v. 4). The union between Jesus and his disciples must also be preserved. Jesus explains what is entailed. The disciples must choose him of their own free will; Jesus will remain if the disciples do. Yet they can do nothing, bear none of the fruit of divine life, without the sap which they get from him. How unfathomable this mystery, but how simply it is expressed.

Jesus had said that he was the vine; now he explicitly tells the disciples, "you are the branches." They must remain constantly with him, just as the branches must remain attached to the vine. Although separation from the vine by sin is not necessarily absolute and final in the spiritual order, separation can become permanent. The worst consequences follow—the separated branches wither away. "Cut off from me you can do nothing" (v. 5). These words strike at the root of pelagianism, which holds in one form or another that (sinful) man can acquire grace by himself by natural means. To be sure, the opposite of activism, quietism, must also be guarded against.

The branches of the vine are judged by their potential to bring forth fruit. If they do not yield fruit, they are the wood of the vine which, being of no practical use (Ez 15:1–5), is good for nothing but burning. Men are threatened by a similar fate. This does not refer to future punishment but is the immediate consequence of separation from Christ. It is a melancholy truth that man can freely turn from Jesus and be lost. Jesus says nothing here about repentance and forgiveness (possible in the spiritual order), because not everything can be said in one image.

Verse 7 contains a practical solution to the mystery of salvation—prayer. The promise is very general; in the context, the disciple should ask only to be saved. "If you remain in me and (if) my words remain in you, ask what you will and it shall be done to you" (v. 7). The prayer of one who remains in Jesus, like the prayer uttered "in his name" (14:13), is sure to be heard. Union with Jesus lends an ever-increasing liberty and universality to prayer. Ask what you will.

"It is to the glory of my Father that you should bear much

fruit, and then you will be my disciples" (v. 8). The glory rendered to God has two causes: the faithful shall bear much fruit, and shall be (future) disciples of Jesus. Jesus seems to be pointing to the future, and if Jesus uttered these words shortly after he had chosen the Twelve, they make a great deal of sense; it was not only after the death of the Savior that the disciples became disciples.

Union with Christ (15:9–17)

Here Jesus drops the figure of the vine but retains the image of fruit. He stresses the idea that the union between the vine and the branches is one of love. The Master's love for his disciples is a kind of friendship, and they must in their turn love others as they would their friends, giving external proof of their love. "As the Father has loved me, so have I loved you; remain in my love" (v. 9). This "remaining" depends upon man's will, so it is made the object of a command. The disciples have only to remain in that love "which God has first had for us, and which moved him to send his Son as a propitiation for our sins" (1 Jn 4:10). Jesus, the model for his disciples, explains: "If you keep my commandments you will remain in my love" (v. 10). We have only to follow his example: "I have kept my Father's commandments, and remain in his love" (v. 10). It need hardly be mentioned that Jesus' obedience to the Father, and that of the disciples who follow him, is continual, and thus another reason why the Father should love them.

The Master tells the disciples all this—that he loves as he is loved, that they should obey as he obeys—because he wants to share his joy with them. "I have told you this so that my joy may be in you, and that your joy be complete" (v. 11). Nothing is more conducive to joy than knowing that one is loved by another. The apostles share the love of Christ. Joy expands the beloved; in happiness, the heart experiences a feeling of fullness (3:29; 16:24; 1 Jn 1:4; Acts 13:52; Rom 15:13). As Leon Bloy wrote, "Joy is the most infallible sign of the presence of God."

In the Semitic mode, one word often leads to another. Thus John's Prologue provides many instances of concatenation— the end of one sentence becomes the beginning of another. For example, "in him was life . . . and the life was the light of men . . . and the light shines in darkness." Having just told his disciples that to remain united to him they were to observe his commandments, Jesus now reduces these commandments to one—love of the brethren. "This is my commandment, love one another as I have loved you" (v. 12). This means much more than some vague affectation of goodwill or a nebulous humanitarianism. If they follow Jesus' example, their love will lead to sacrifice, for he will give his life for them and for all mankind. Men have been known to die for their friends. "A man can have no greater love than to lay down his life for his friends" (v. 13). Jesus alludes here to his own death, although nothing in the context would indicate that it is imminent. The phrase has about it the ring of a proverbial saying.

The word "friend" leads to the word "friends." One cannot speak of love for others without including the notion of friendship, for love is a kind of friendship. In fact, it is because the disciples obey that they are friends, for their obedience is the condition of their remaining in his love. He is Lord and Master, which implies that they are servants or slaves. However, "I no longer speak of you as slaves" (v. 15). Servant and friend are not mutually exclusive terms, since friendship does not exclude the idea of service. But there is this difference: the slave obeys without knowing the purpose of his master's actions, while friends share in his knowledge and are admitted to his confidence. Thus Jesus declares, "I call you friends, since I have made known to you all that I heard from my Father" (v. 15).

The "all" is surprising there, especially in view of 16:12, where Jesus says that there are many things still to be revealed. However, the revelation of "all things" depended upon the will of the Father. Jesus has revealed all that the Father had commissioned him to reveal up to this moment.

In calling his disciples "friends," Jesus does not suppress all distinction of rank; they are still servants. Abraham was the "friend of God" (Is 41:8; 2 Chr 20:7; Jas 2:23). In Arabic, Abraham is called El-Khalil, which means The Friend of God. The New Testament ideal is to be the friend of Christ. The apostles had done nothing to deserve the honor of this friendship, but the time had come for it. Jesus has finished giving them personal teaching and training. Now he reveals the significance of what he has done.

The disciples may have thought that in leaving their nets and boats and counting tables, the decision had been their own. Now Jesus claims the initiative even there: "It was not you who chose me, it was I who chose you" (v. 16). Luke observed that Jesus had chosen the Twelve after a night of prayer (6:13). Mark supplies the reason: they were to be his companions whom he would send to preach the good news (3:14). In his gospel, John repeatedly expresses the gratuitous character of the divine call without in any way suggesting that the Apostles' personal liberty and responsibility were diminished. Jesus elevated his disciples to the dignity of being his friends, but this in no way deprived him of his right to command. Thus he provides them with a definite program for apostolic action. They were "to go forth and bear fruit, and your fruit must remain" (v. 16).

Thus the key to this discourse is apostolic action. The prospects which Christ opens up before them—of going in his name to do his work while following his way—are global in extent. To Galilean fishermen, this future must have been staggering, making them aware of their awesome responsibility. They will produce the "fruit that remains," not by their own natural activity, but thanks to the prayers they utter in union with Jesus: "all you ask the Father in my name he will give you" (v. 16). When in the Sermon on the Mount Jesus had said, "Ask and you shall receive," he implied that such asking would have to fulfill certain conditions, the chief of which would be, "Thy will be done." Prayer will help them carry out the divine program. The Father remains distinct from the Son here, as he does throughout this section; the trinitarian doctrine is less clearly defined than in chapter 14, which took up the matter of the union of the Father and the Son. Here it is the Father, not the Son, who answers prayers.

"The command I give you is this, that you love one another" (v. 17). The one command is, oddly enough, referred to by a plural "these things" (*tauta*). This simply makes the command all the more striking: as if Jesus had said, "this is all that I command you." Everything comes down to this—fraternal charity.

Hatred of the World (15:18–25)

The fact that the disciples are united with their Master and friend, and obey him in loving one another, means that they share his lot: "you find that the world hates you, know it has hated me before you" (v. 18). Jesus gives three reasons why his beloved disciples shall be hated. First, they are so radically different in character from the world. "The world" means the hostile Jewish world, and all who have not welcomed Christ. Friendship supposes a common ground, and this is lacking between the world and the apostles. The apostles are signs of contradiction, different from the world. The world therefore counters with hostility. "Because you do not belong to the world . . . the world hates you" (v. 19).

Jesus continues: "Remember what I told you: no slave is greater than his master" (v. 20). This admonition repeats 13:16, and is thus surprising; would the Apostles have so soon forgotten what the Lord had said after he had washed their feet? The present discourse has probably been inserted here out of its chronological order. Jesus expressed the same idea in his teaching about the apostolate (Mt. 10:24). The allusion is less to 13:16 than to a well-known bit of the Master's advice (cf. Lk 6:40).

The second reason for the world's hatred is the apostles' mission: "They will harry you as they harried me. They will respect your words as much as they respected mine" (v. 20). The disciples must be ready for persecution, and also for the indifference and negligence of those whom they shall instruct.

Finally, the disciples shall be hated simply because they are Christ's disciples. Presenting themselves in Christ's name, they shall receive the same kind of welcome he did. "But all this they will do to you because of my name, for they know nothing of him who sent me" (v. 21). Unbelievers do not see because they insist on keeping their eyes closed (16:3). "If I had not come to them and spoken to them, they would not be guilty of sin; now, however, their sin cannot be excused" (v. 22). Not to understand the mission of Christ is not to know the Father. The same doctrine has been expressed in chapter 14, where the unity between the Father and Son is more fully stated than here. The reason for hatred is this: "To hate me is to hate my Father" (v. 23).

Jesus came not in words only, but in deeds as well. In 14:11 the "works" prove the unity of the Father and the Son; here they prove his mission. The world does not hate the Father in the Son, but it hates the Son *and* the Father—two persons. "Had I not performed such works among them as no one has ever done before, they would not be guilty of sin. But now they have seen, and they go on hating me and my Father" (v. 24). The prophets had performed miracles, but Jesus' work defies description, or at least comparison. John uses the word *erga* here—"work" instead of his usual term "sign"—in referring to all that Jesus did. The perfection of Jesus' work made it shine out.

Future Persecutions (15:26—16:4)

Hatred for the Messiah had been foretold in the Law, using Law in the wide sense so as to include the Psalms. The Law contained the words, "they have hated me without cause" (Ps 34:19; 68:5), but this had been overlooked. However, Jesus says, neither the infidelity of the Chosen People nor the world's hostility can impede the power of God. Jesus will send a Defender who will, along with apostles of all ages, bear witness to the truth of Jesus' teachings.

That the Holy Spirit is not an "it" but a person is deducible from the words Jesus used in describing him and his mission. He said, "When the Counselor comes, whom I shall send to you from the Father . . . "(15:26). The Greek article and pronoun are anything but neuter. The Holy Spirit will be sent by Jesus, and from the very bosom of the Father. He will be a faithful messenger, knowledgeable in all divine secrets. Jesus' assurance ("I shall send") stems from his own divinity, and is a decidedly divine gesture, for no creature or mere man could send a divine person.

With the words, "The Spirit of Truth who proceeds from the Father," we are deep into the mystery of the Trinity. The spirit proceeds from the Father by an eternal, not a temporal procession; his testimony, then, has a clearly defined character and authority. But the world cannot and will not receive him, for he cannot be seen and touched, or quantified in any fashion.

Jesus says, "He will bear witness to me" (v. 26). There are many ways of bearing witness in the Fourth Gospel; among them are the preaching of the Baptist, the words of Jesus himself, the voice of the Father at the Jordan and on Mt. Thabor, and the words of the evangelist himself. Once Jesus ascends into heaven, the Spirit will take his place and continue his witness. "The Spirit is the witness because the Spirit is the truth" (1 Jn 5:7). The earlier witness was geared to the world, so to speak; the later witness will be an interior one. "And you also are witnesses," Jesus continued, "because you have been with me from the beginning" (v. 27). (There is much food for thought in the fact that the Greek word for "witness" is "martyr.") The good news was to be handed down by the apostles who had been with Jesus when he spoke, and as he performed his miracles. Just the same, the Spirit will help them penetrate the heart of Jesus' teachings (16:13) and instil in them the courage to proclaim that news to the ends of the earth (Acts 1:8).

Jesus had frequently warned his disciples that they would often preach to unreceptive hearers. They would learn soon enough by experience the incredulity and hostility of the world and of its scorn for a doctrine that demanded so much of man. Few things can shake one's confidence more than scorn and derision. Seeing that Israel rejected him, the apostles might be tempted to wonder whether Jesus was in fact God's envoy to the Chosen People. But even the hatred which the apostles would inherit after Jesus' death was part of God's plan; he braced them for what was coming: "I have said all this to you to keep you from falling away. They will put you out of the synagogues . . . whoever kills you will think he is offering service to God" (16:1–2). Christians all over the world today are experiencing the truth of Jesus' words.

One wonders at the paradox of divine wisdom. Imagine entrusting to men a mission that would lead to their humiliation and disgrace! Yet that is what lay ahead for the apostles. Expulsion from the synagogue was the equivalent of excommunication. For God-fearing Jews, this punishment was little short of death. It meant being cut off, excluded from one's own nation (see Jn 9:22; 12:42), being judged unworthy of membership in it by God-fearing people. Death too was a distinct possibility; Stephen would be the first to go, then James, and then Peter.

Those who persecuted the apostles and the Church were usually sincere men animated by a darksome zeal (Rom 10:2). Spiritual blindness is common; when it is deliberate it becomes damnable. Jesus had brought a light into the world, and it was spurned. "They will do this because they have not known the Father, nor me" (v. 3). What was this light? It was the revelation that Jesus was the incarnate Son of God. Monotheism is also a light, but Christianity brings with it a great flood of light. Candles give light, but the sun at midday puts out the candles.

Jesus had withheld knowledge of this somewhat depressing future from his disciples until now, at the end. While he was alive, he had been the target; now they will draw the fire of hostile critics. "I have said these things to you that when their hour comes, you may remember that I told you of them" (v. 4). He had in fact touched on all this before (Mt 5:10–12) but never so clearly. He is going away, but he promises to send the Holy Spirit (vv. 5–15); he will himself return and fill them with joy (vv. 16–24); their faith in him will in the end be triumphant over the world (vv. 25–33).

Jesus' Departure (16:4–33)

The Promise of the Holy Spirit (5–15)

The knowledge that Jesus was going to his Father brought little comfort to the apostles, who had grown accustomed to the Master's presence and guidance. They were not particularly impressed that they would gain by his going. After all, a bird in the hand. . . . But really the situation called for joy, not sorrow. "I tell you the truth: it is to your advantage that I go away, for if I do not go away, the Counselor will not come to you; but if I go, I will send him to you (v. 7).

It was not part of God's plan to send the Counselor so long as Jesus remained on earth. The reward of his passion and death would be precisely this incredible gift. If Jesus had remained upon earth, most of his followers would have settled for his bodily presence. Far better would be the invisible presence of his Spirit, unhampered by such things as time and space. As a result of his Spirit's presence, Jesus would never be far from his disciples or from the Holy Spirit (with whom he is inseparably one). While they walk in faith, deprived of his bodily presence, their faith will be exercised and purified until they better understand the meaning of his words.

Thus St. Dominic assured his brethren that he would be more helpful to them in heaven, interceding for them, than he would be upon earth. St. Thérèse of Lisieux spoke in similar fashion to her sisters in the Carmelite Order.

Jesus' next words evoke the setting of a legal trial. In juridical terms he describes the role the Spirit will play in the future (vv. 8–11). His words are quite obscure to us, but they were meant to help the disciples view the events which were soon to follow, in the proper way. He was referring to his own coming condemnation. The Spirit, like an able defense attorney, will convict the world of its mistaken judgment concerning Jesus.

The world which Jesus refers to here is that world whose prince is Satan (12:31; 14:30), the world of those who prefer darkness to the light (3:20; Eph 5:11). This world would cry out that Jesus was guilty (7:49), a sinner (9:24), a blasphemer (10:33), a troublemaker (18:30), and accursed (cf. Dt 21:23; Gal 3:13) since he had died on a cross. The charges were formidable, yet they will all be met and the first verdict overturned. When seen in the proper light it will be clear that, (1) sin is on the side of the world; (2) justice is on the side of Jesus; and (3) that the only one truly condemned is Satan (vv. 8–11).

Apart from this "legal" aspect, the Holy Spirit will be the great educator. There was a need for this. Jesus had (despite 15:15) departed before the disciples were fully instructed. Revelation is, after all, a progressive process on God's part, and an assimilative one on man's. Truth is always on the march and growth in it is a sign of life. Simply because it becomes more complete, truth does not cease to be truth. Was Jesus perhaps not here alerting his disciples to beware of rigidity of teaching which would run counter to the normal processes of thought? He promised that "the Spirit of truth . . . will guide you into all truth" (vv. 12, 13). The Greek verb here implies movement along a road toward (the preposition used indicates motion) the truth. Jesus had made the astonishing statement: "I am the way . . . " (14:6), and the disciples would have to suffer for teaching "the way." It was a way that went somewhere, that led to a greater understanding of the old truths—and of the new ones still to be revealed up to the death of the last apostle. And after that? Teaching authority resides in the Church, and Jesus' promise includes the assistance that will always be given to the successors of the apostles (14:16). With the help of the Holy Spirit, they will penetrate ever more deeply into the truths of revelation, learning more about the messianic kingdom, about the nature of the Church, and of God himself.

The divine counselor will be a substitute for Jesus, but not a competitor or rival. He will not set forth doctrines peculiar to himself, but will rather confirm what Jesus had said. "He will not speak on his own authority, but whatever he hears he will speak, and he will declare to you the things that are to come" (v. 13). Jesus had not spoken of himself, either, but of the Father. The Spirit will guide the Church in her perception of the things new and old to be found in tradition and the gospels.

Jesus and the Paraclete teach the same truths, which derive from a source common to them both—the Father. What the Spirit receives from the Father, he also receives from the Son who possesses all that the Father does (17:10). Nowhere else in the gospel is the unity of nature and distinction of persons in the Trinity so clearly stated as in 16:13–14. "All that the Father has is mine; therefore I said that he will take what is mine and declare it to you" (v. 15). Christian theology also sees in these words (vv. 14–15) the doctrine concerning the procession which unites the Spirit to the Father and to the Son.

Jesus Will Return (16:16–23)

Another reason for the joy lying ahead of the apostles is the return of their Master. It will be a matter of a few short hours. The phrase "a little while" is used seven times. "A little while and you will see me no more" (note the euphemism for "death"); "again a little while and you will see me" (v. 16). If he was going to the Father (v. 17) (the words sounded quite final), why then should he come back at all? The apostles' confusion extends to the readers of these verses. Will his coming back be at the end of time, which compared to eternity will be only a moment hence? Or do the words mean "after the resurrection"? The second opinion is the better, for Jesus went on to assure them that their sorrow would be of short duration. Weep and lament they might, but like the pangs of childbirth which are quickly transmuted, their sadness will soon turn into joy. Jesus will come again and they will see him (vv. 19–22). Here he does not promise them eternal joy, but a spiritual joy. "Your hearts" (once considered as the seat of the emotions) "will rejoice" (v. 22). Jesus has died once and for all; the joy he brings will have no seasons but will last. "No one will take your joy away for you. . . . And then there will be no need for further questions" (vv. 22, 23).

Prayer Is Always Heard (16:23–33)

With Jesus' two magnificent promises ringing in their ears, the disciples' confidence grew. Jesus would return, and the Holy Spirit would help them. Now Jesus assures them that the Father is well-disposed toward them and will hear their prayers.

Up to this moment, the disciples had done remarkable things in Jesus' name, but they had not used his name when they prayed to the Father. Jesus now directs them to do so; their prayers will thus have greater efficacy than before. Prayer in Jesus' name is an appeal to his power as mediator and as the divine Son who is able and willing to do what they ask him (14:13). The Church has obeyed this command, ending countless prayers with the words, ". . . through Jesus Christ our Lord."

To pray to the Father through the Son was a revolutionary teaching. Jesus had prayed to his Father; so had they. But from now on, their prayers will be unlike those of ancient Israel, for they will be directed to God through the divine highpriest who has entered, once and for all, into the Holy of Holies (Heb 10:19f). "Hitherto you have asked nothing in my name; ask, and you will receive, that your joy may be full" (v. 24).

Up to this moment, Jesus had spoken in a language obscure and difficult to understand. "I have said this to you in figures. The hour is coming when I shall speak to you . . . plainly of the Father" (v. 25). After the resurrection and Pentecost, he spoke both through himself and the Spirit about the Father, and grace, and glory. And here is an interesting fact—no limits are set to the progressive fulfillment of this promise. The Spirit began its working at Pentecost, and will continue in every age of the Church. We are in fact living in the era of the Spirit, as the charismatic movement clearly shows.

Once the Advocate has come, the apostles were to pray in Jesus' name. Jesus' next words must have been perplexing to them: "I do not say to you that I shall pray to the Father for you" (v. 26). Jesus meant that from Pentecost on, the apostles would be so united to him in faith and love that when they prayed, he would pray in them. They will need no introduction to the Father other than their love for his Son, and his name upon their lips. The Father who loves his Son also loves those who are one with that Son. The disciples will need no one to present their prayers to the Father, for their prayers are those of his own beloved Son. They will have "the mind of Christ," and will only ask what Jesus would ask.

This revelation of the intimate union that exists between Jesus and his own, a union based on love and faith, marks a high point in Christian mysticism. Our spiritual efforts and strivings should all be aimed at that union with Jesus which guarantees direct contact with God the Father. The apostles believed that Jesus "came from the Father" (v. 27); he for his part unites them, and all men, to the Father, for he is the eternal mediator (Rom 8:34; Heb 8:6; 9:24; 1 Jn 2:1). Even now, he intercedes for them in glory.

"I came from the Father and have come into the world again, I am leaving the world and going to the Father" (v. 28). The two stages of Jesus' odyssey of redemption are (1) his divine origin or departure from the Father in the Incarnation, and (2) his return by way of his death and ascension. There are resonances here with 13:3, and Isaiah 55:11: "My word shall not return to me empty," but with its mission accomplished.

Now this sort of talk made sense, the apostles thought. Now you are talking sense, they as good as told him. "Now we know that you know all things, and need none to question you; by this we believe that you came from God" (v. 30). They thought they understood completely. But Jesus had promised a perfect understanding that would only come much later on. The apostles were sincere and enthusiastic, but their faith had as yet little depth or strength. Jesus knew how to evaluate it. "The hour is coming . . . when you will be scattered . . . and will leave me alone. Yet I am not alone, for the Father is with me" (v. 32). Human friends would soon desert him, but the Father would not fail him, not even on the Cross. Far from needing the support of the apostles, Jesus will himself be their strength in the trials to come.

"I have said this to you, that in me you may have peace. In the world you have tribulation; but be of good cheer, I have overcome the world (v. 33). The contrast between "In me . . . peace," and "in the world . . . affliction," is startling. Christ's peace is not based upon the premise that there will be no external trials, but upon the certain confidence of triumph with Jesus himself. His personal victory spells the final victory of all who are united to him. Jesus' last words to the disciples are splendid and thrilling: "Be brave," or "Have courage! I have overcome the world." Throughout the gospel, Jesus is constantly urging people to have courage, not to be afraid: the paralytic and the woman with the flow of blood, the apostles in the midst of the storm at sea, Paul later on in chains (Acts 23:11).

Christ has conquered the world! There is a great mystery here. For Jesus alone, the victory is complete and definitive; for the apostles there is hardship ahead. But they must nevertheless be confident in their leader. "In all trials, we are more than conquerors through him who loved us," Paul would write (Rom 8:37).

These are Jesus' final words to his apostles, a stirring ending to a marvelous discourse. Jesus goes to his death with a shout of triumph on his lips, urging his followers to face the future with courage. Peace, affliction, courage, and victory, are the four thoughts he leaves them with in this solemn conclusion to his last earthly conversation with them.

John 17: The Great Highpriestly Prayer

John 17 contains the only long, continuous prayer of Jesus recorded in the New Testament. It was uttered at the Last Supper following the famous discourses of chapters 13–16, and forms a moving introduction to the passion which begins in chapter 18. The strands of this prayer are: love, knowledge, eternal life, glory, and oneness, and they are skillfully woven together. The artless simplicity of the words has not deceived the great saints, who saw in Jesus' words the perfect description of the spiritual life. To know God, to love him, to be aware of his presence within the thinker and the lover, to be one with him in some mysterious but real fashion—these are traits that have distinguished all the great mystics and all true servants of the Lord.

The closing verses of John 16 paint a picture of a joyful Christ, exulting in the completion of his mision and certain that the apostles will carry it on. Jesus turned to his Father in this prayer (called the great highpriestly prayer) to ask his assistance for the disciples. One recalls the prayer of Onias in 2 Mc 15:12. Jesus, the perfect victim, was prepared to die; in him the ancient Jewish feast of Yom Kippur, the great day of expiation, was to find its perfect fulfillment. Even more so than Aaron (Wis 18:21f), Jesus became the champion of his people, bearing the weapons of his special office—prayer and atonement.

This great prayer is a Semitic masterpiece, and therefore not an ordered, systematic treatise. It may however be divided as follows:

1. Jesus prays for himself   vv. 1–8
2. Jesus prays for his disciples   vv. 9–19
3. Jesus prays for the Church   vv. 20–23
4. Conclusion to the prayer   vv. 24–26

Jesus' Prayer for Himself (vv. 1–8)

The great highpriestly prayer was first heard in the Upper Room. There "Jesus lifted his eyes heavenward." It is natural for us to think and speak of God in terms of "height," just as we speak of various excellent human traits in that way (high honors, a high I.Q., etc.). By contrast, baseness or inferiority of any kind is described as being low (low standards, low brow, etc.). Addressing his heavenly Father, Jesus proclaimed: "The hour has come!" The "hour" is his passion. Long anticipated, for many years a "not yet," it has finally become a "now." For both Jesus and all mankind, it is a momentous hour, and Jesus faced it with a great serenity and joy. The die is cast, as it were, and he knows he will carry out the charge laid upon him. It will involve moments of great suffering; he will endure it. Gethsemani and the cross will be a fearful trial, but the real struggle and victory were won first of all upon the field of the spirit by divine power. And Jesus has made the choice. Human enough to go from exaltation to sadness, he will hold firm.

"Glorify your Son, that your Son may glorify you" (v. 1). Here are two requests: that the Father again show his love for his Son, and that the passion of that Son might bring glory to the Father. Jesus had spent his life seeking to promote his Father's glory (11:4; 13:31). He had carried out the task he had been assigned, it could not have been done better. Confidently then, he asks that this "hour" become an occasion of glory for himself, that is, that he be accepted and recognized and honored by the Father. Unless this happened, the sacrifice on Calvary would not contribute to the Father's glory. The Father did accept him, of course, for as Paul writes, "Being born in human form . . . obediently accepting even death, death on a cross . . . God has highly exalted him (Phil 2:7–9).

The word "glory" is a word of "splendor." It is a thoroughly biblical word associated with the Lord's power and majesty (Ex 24:16). But glory is not something that shines in the dark; it is linked with public recognition and praise, and with fulsome approval.

"You have given him (Jesus) power over all flesh" (v. 2). The Incarnate Son has received from his Father a power over all "flesh," a term that describes mankind in its weakness and frailty. With this power, Jesus "gave eternal life to all whom you gave him" (v. 2). A Savior without power to save is nonsense. Jesus had that power (3:35; 10:10), but the universality and extent of his power would only be manifest after he had entered into glory. Once he was exalted, the limitations of his earthly ministry in time and space would be overcome and the negligible number of his followers would become many. Tertullian gave magnificent expression to the truth of these words.

John had stated that the Son had the power to give eternal life and to pronounce sentence upon men (5:19–30). Here (17:3) he explains what that life is. "This is eternal life: to know you, the only true God, and Jesus Christ, whom you have sent (v. 3). Eternal life, then, is linked with knowing God and Jesus Christ. But this knowing must be understood in a Semitic mode. The Old Testament does not evince any great interest in intellectual things. When it is stated in the Bible that Abraham "knew" his wife, it means more than that he knew her name was Sarah. Love and knowledge become almost interchangeable. To know someone implies a kind of recognition and intimacy with another which finds its expression in love (Hos 2:20; 6:6). But knowledge is also, as John here says, bound up with faith, and involves an acceptance of Jesus Christ.

One does not accept half a man. To know or to accept Jesus Christ is to accept the whole Christ—person and teachings. Knowledge of Jesus Christ becomes a way of life, a loving fulfillment of his commandments (14:15, 21). To know God is to have eternal life; to know Christ is to possess that life. One does not have to acquire two knowledges, for Jesus is both the way to God, and the end of the journey as well.

"I have glorified you on earth by finishing the work you

gave me to do" (v. 4). What a special, but immense, satisfaction it is to complete a difficult assignment. Jesus had done so, intent only on enhancing the glory of the Father. The divine plan of salvation reveals how good and how loving and how deserving of glory the Father is. Jesus, poised on the threshold of his passion, knows that he will carry it through. His atoning death is as good as done. He confidently asks for the reward due such a death, namely, that in God's own presence, "the Father will glorify me with the glory I had with you before the world was made" (v. 5). These words are an astonishing claim to pre-existence, and in them there are resonances of John 1:1–4; 2 Cor 8:9; Phil 2:5ff. Before the world was made, he had known glory; now he asks that, once his human existence has ended, his assumed human nature be also associated with him in rightful glory. Faithfulness to one's charge or mission calls for a suitable reward. In this case, Jesus asks that the splendor of the victorious Son radiate out upon his human nature. God seems incredibly intent upon restoring human nature to dignity and honor—even to glory.

Jesus next recalled the relationship that existed between himself and the apostles. They were his Father's gift to the incarnate Son, and to them Jesus revealed his Father's name. In Semitic usage, to know a person's name was to know that person; the two went together. He told them all about the Father, and they slowly came to realize that the Father was the Lord, and that Jesus who was one with the Father was also Lord. He was the envoy God sent from his very bosom. No other prophet or messenger was ever so described. Jesus could say then that "they know that everything you have given me is from you; for I have given them the words which you gave me, and they have received them, and know in truth that I came from you" (vv. 7–8). Jesus' errand of redemption became known, and its result was the creation of the Church made up of real men drawn from the world by the power of God.

Jesus Prays for his Disciples (17:9–19).

The apostles were few in number. A slender harvest perhaps, but enough to bring joy to Jesus' heart. They are the new society committed to the proclamation of his saving message and the continuation of the work of the Incarnate word. Since they were the first to believe in him as God's Son, they held a privileged place in his heart. "I pray for them," he said, ". . . for those whom you have given me. All mine are yours, and yours are mine, and I am glorified in them" (vv. 9–10). In the tender intimacy of these last moments, Jesus prayed especially for those who had accepted him. The glory of Jesus will shine through the ages, and the whole world will benefit from their loyalty, if they persevere in their witness to him. The Father, who in his wisdom and providence gave the apostles to Jesus, now has a twofold reason for watching over them—they belong both to him and to his beloved Son.

By honoring Jesus as their master and by following him at some risk to themselves, the apostles had glorified him. "I am glorified in them" (17:10; 13:13). Their desertion of him in Gethsemani will illustrate the fragility of their belief, but Jesus saw beyond that; they were the firstfruits of his mission, and in time they would make him known to all. They were good men, these friends. The future would prove their worth.

"And now I am no more in the world, but they are" (v. 11). Jesus will soon leave the disciples and return to his Father, and the disciples will be buffeted by human discord and self-will. Without his visible presence to strengthen them, they will know what indecision is. In order to overcome such trials, Jesus prayed to the Father to help them. The world is a hostile place, an arena in which the forces of good and evil are in constant conflict. Even so, Jesus does not reject it, for he is going to die for *all* men, excluding none (3:16; Lk 23:34).

What Jesus asks of the Father for his disciples is a great gift—holiness. He addressed his Father by an unusual title: "Holy Father!" Holiness is an attribute of God. It suggests separation from earthly things and a transcendence so absolute as to evoke filial fear. But holiness is communicable, and it is the mark of all true disciples of Jesus. It is a quality or tone of life which enables the possessor to approach God with the confidence of a friend. God's friends, the saints, may live in a profane world, but they are not part of it.

"Keep them in your name, which you have given me" (v. 11). Here is John at his provocative best. What is Jesus saying? He is asking that the Father protect the disciples, and keep them steadfast in their belief. The words "in your name" reflect a Semitic mind-set quite different from the western mentality. Jewish reverence for the divine name was so profound that the word "Yahweh" was never pronounced; YHWH was and is the sacred tetragrammaton (the four holy letters). I recall vividly how in our classes at the Ecole Biblique de Jérusalem, a German Jewish lad would automatically substitute for YHWH the words "The Name." "Father" was the name Jesus the Son revealed. It brings together the worship of the Father and the Son (12:28; 14:8–11; 17:3–6, 26) and is a sign of their unity. Jesus prayed that the disciples reflect that same unity, and know the love and understanding that stems from this divine model (3:16–18; 1 Jn 4:8–16). The apostles would not always see eye-to-eye about the proper way to preach the gospel (cf. Acts 11:2; Gal 2:11), but their basic unity of belief helped them resolve their differences. The plurality of persons (Father and Son) is not disruptive of the divine unity, and in some way the separate existences of Christians who make up the body of Christ (here seen but dimly) blend harmoniously in the oneness of belief.

"While I was with them, I kept them in your name" (v. 12). Jesus had successfully held the Twelve together, with the sole exception of "the one who chose to be lost" (2 Thes 2:3; Mt 23:15). Judas was the one "destined to be lost, that the scripture might be fulfilled." Both Christians and Jews have taught that one becomes a "son of the kingdom" by choice, and not by nature. One can turn from God or toward him, as simply as one can blot out or let in the light of the sun. More will be said about Judas and his fate in a later chapter. The scriptures Jesus refers to here are probably Ps 41:10; 55:13ff, and Jn 13:18.

Jesus prayed aloud, and the apostles took heart at his words. They realized that they would be protected by Jesus' loving Father and by the Master as well, only now from on high. Addressing his Father, Jesus continues, "Now I am coming to you; I say all this while I am still in the world that they may share my joy completely" (v. 13). However, they would shortly find themselves targets of persistent hostility, and they needed such consoling words. "The world hated them because they are not of the world, even as I am not of the world" (v. 14). Because the world—everything that is not of Christ—hates the light (15:18ff), they need protection from the world. This "world" reacts against those who do not conform to it (7:7; 15:19), and rejects the idea that there is more to life than the natural world. Jesus had laid down the ultimate challenge. He had proclaimed that his heavenly Father was and is knowable in the person and teachings of his Son, and that one comes to know the Father by knowing the Son.

Why does the "world" find this message so distasteful? Probably because of what is implied in Jesus' words: that God is the Supreme Being (not man), that Jesus is God-in-the-flesh, that man's sins are displeasing to God and must be settled for, and that worldly standards are too limited and short-sighted for the sons and daughters of God.

To be hated by anyone is a horrible experience. The disciples could be spared this only by somehow fleeing the world. Jesus did not want that, for he prayed as follows: "I do not want you to take them out of the world, but to keep them from the evil one" (v. 15). It is precisely the evil world that constitutes the proper field of apostolic action. If the apostles were to leave the world with Jesus, his work would have died with him. He therefore prayed, not that they be isolated from the world, nor that they be spared persecution, sacrifice, and struggle, nor that they be deprived of seeing their faith victorious, but only that the Father keep them from the evil one. Let the Father take care of those who live as his Son had lived, in the world but not of it. "They are not of the world, even as I am not of the world" (v. 16). Looking back over history, one can see how the Church has affected the world, and essentially has never been affected by it. Jesus' prayer has been effective.

Thus far, Jesus has asked his heavenly Father to keep the apostles together in unity and to resist the sometimes fascinating but always corrosive power of evil. Next he asked for them a great spirit of dedication and holiness. "Consecrate them in the truth; your word is truth" (v. 17). The Greek word used here (*hagiazo*), refers to a consecration or dedication to God of an unblemished, sacrificial victim; the word is often synonymous with sacrifice (Ex 13:2; Dt 16:19, 21; 27:19). Jesus has already asked his Father that his followers be holy men preserved from the contagion of the world. Their consecration, which he now asks, will complete their separation from the world and knit them more closely to God. "Truth" in the Old Testament usage means a good moral life perfectly attuned to God's will. Contrasted to it are moral error—injustice and sin. Truth means fidelity, loyalty, reliability, keeping one's promises. God keeps his promises, and the men who live out the truth are living the faith. They are of the truth who believe it, who love it, who walk in its ways, who do it. Jesus prays that the apostles not be mere speakers of the truth, but men dedicated to it and interiorly transformed by it.

"As you have sent me into the world, so I have sent them into the world" (v. 18). With these words, Jesus commissions his apostles to carry on the task he came into the world to perform. Jesus sanctifies himself, that is, he is ready to immolate himself for them. He is consecrated to God, a dedicated priest and victim. The disciples must enter into and share in his state as victim; their holiness comes from his holiness (v. 19). His love and his death will inspire them.

History has shown that Jesus' prayer for his apostles was effective, for after the descent of the Holy Spirit, they went forth preaching the truth throughout the world. The Lord cooperated with them too, confirming their words with signs and wonders. Finally, all of them (except John) would die martyrs' deaths for the truth of his word.

Jesus Prays for the Church (17:20–23)

The expressions which Jesus used here need not be understood exclusively of later times or later institutions. Jesus was praying for his immediate disciples, asking that the unity he has already prayed for be a reality among them. His prayer was directed first of all toward a unity reflecting that of the

Father and the Son; then to their union with the Father and the Son; and finally, a petition that this unity would induce the world to believe in him and his mission.

"I do not pray for these only, but also for those who believe in me through their word" (v. 20). The ministry, far from being something secret, was to be shouted from the housetops, repeated over and over in a multitude of circumstances. Paul would write:

> How are men to call upon him in whom they have not believed? And how are they to believe in him of whom they have never heard? And how are they to hear without a preacher? As it is written, "How beautiful are the feet of those who preach good news!" (Rom 10:14–15)

"That they may all be one; even as you Father, are in me, and I in you, that they also may be in us, so that the world may believe that you sent me" (v. 21). Preaching is designed to bring about a mystical union between believers and their God. Preachers are not mere instructors, but men who desire their listeners to attain a union with God similar to that of the Father and the Son. The way to God is not through ecstasy, but through a faith that has been aroused by the public testimony of the apostles. Such a faith involves commitment, the reception of the sacraments, and the giving of oneself to the promptings of the Holy Spirit.

"The glory which you have given me I have given to them" (v. 22). John has frequently spoken of glory (*doxa*). It is a property of the divine nature which, to men, is something light or lightsome or splendid. It shines forth, both in Jesus and in the life of his Church, by outward manifestations such as miracles and supernatural signs. Surpassingly great is the honor of Christ's followers, to whom he has given of his glory so as to unify them, "that they may be one, even as we are one" (v. 22). Jesus and his disciples are united in a profound, mysterious way, and as he has remained ever united with his heavenly Father, those who are one with him are also one with the

Father, loved by him even as Jesus is loved (v. 23). Here is the very heart of the mystic's unitive way.

Conclusion (17:24–26)

In this dramatic conclusion, Jesus twice invokes the Father. The horizon opens wide so as to include all the faithful. The background is that of eternal life. "Father, I desire that these men, who are your gift to me, may be with me where I am" (v. 24). Jesus does not ask this favor but seems almost to demand it (the verb "desire" indicates a great intensity); he defers to his Father but with a calm confidence that his prayer will be heard. He is going to prepare a place for them (14:3), and it affords him pleasure to have his own with him at that moment.

"To behold my glory, which you have given me" (v. 24). The Father's gifts and call are irrevocable (Rom 11:29). Jesus desires that his disciples may with him gaze upon that glory which the Father from all eternity had determined that his Son should have. "Because you loved me before the foundation of the world" (v. 24). It is rather strange that Jesus should now ask that his disciples see the glory which (v. 22) he had just given them, but we are dealing here with a profound reality. Jesus' glory is given to his own, in this life, by grace; it will shine resplendent in the souls of those who preserve it, unto eternal life.

Turning to the concrete needs of his disciples, Jesus addresses him as his Just, or righteous Father. He seems enraptured at the thought of God's holiness and justice, and pauses to contemplate it. "The world has not known you, but I have known you" (v. 25). The sinful world has earned its judgment, but Jesus gazes upon the other side of the picture. "I have known you, and these [my disciples] have known that you have sent me" (v. 25). He who had always claimed to have special knowledge about the Father (7:29; 8:55; 10:15), has shared that knowledge with those who believed in him.

"I made known to them your name, and I will make it known" (v. 26). His death and resurrection will not interrupt his manifesting the Father to the disciples and their successors.

Behind this continued revelation is his desire that "the love with which you have loved me may be in them and I in them." On this loving note, the prayer ends. His final petition is that all may share in the love existing between the Father and the Son. Jesus' departure from them will be his glorification by way of the passion. He will be forever with his Church in love and unity.

CHAPTER FOUR

The Agony in the Garden

The agony in the garden represents the great crisis in Jesus' life. It is vividly described, but with a disconcerting lack of emotion, and the account is all the more impressive for being thus muted. Christians of all denominations instinctively turn to Jesus when they are burdened with sorrow. They derive comfort from the realization that God's own Son knew what suffering was like. Because Jesus suffered so fearfully, we know that suffering does not necessarily mean that God is angry with the sufferer. Indeed, suffering may be, as in Jesus' case, a prelude to great spiritual blessings.

After the Last Supper and the institution of the Eucharist, Jesus and his disciples sang the prescribed Hallel, or psalms of praise (Ps 113–118). They then left the Upper Room and headed for the Mount of Olives. We can literally retrace their steps. Leaving the Cenacle, they made their way down the stepped street (this was re-discovered a hundred years ago and is in daily use today) into the valley of Gehinnom. Proceeding in an easterly direction they soon reached the deep Kidron Valley (Kidron means "dark.") Turning northward they passed the tomb of Absalom on their right, and came to a garden which Matthew and Mark call by name—Gethsemani, which means oil-press. Luke calls it simply "the place." John speaks of a garden across the valley, and on the lower slopes of the Mount of Olives. It is possible that Jesus knew the owner, and had previously made use of the garden. Judas would know where to find him.

Toward the end of the fourth century, the emperor Theodosius had a church built over the place where Jesus suffered his agony. This church and the later Crusader edifice built on the site were both destroyed. The basilica that now adorns the site was constructed after World War I, when the Holy Land was opened to visitors after 400 years of Turkish domination. This building is known as the Church of All Nations since it was put up with alms gathered from all over Christendom. In front of the main altar is a rectangular square of bedrock believed to be the spot where Jesus endured his agony. It is surrounded by an artistic grill. On the north side of the basilica is the garden itself. In it stand eight huge olive trees estimated to be at least 900 years old. The Roman historian Pliny once observed the "olive trees are immortal," and these are in fact, like olive trees everywhere, gnarled and twisted and incredibly tenacious of life. However, when Titus was besieging Jerusalem (66–70 A.D.), he cut down all trees in the neighborhood of the walls, so as to make escape more difficult if not entirely impossible. These trees, then, did not witness the agony.

After leading his disciples into the garden, Jesus paused to say: "Stay here while I go over there and pray" (Mt 26:36). The words "over there" must have been reassuring. He went on a bit further with Peter, James, and John, who had been with him when he raised Jairus' daughter to life (Mk 5:37ff) and when he was transfigured on Mount Thabor. They were now to witness Jesus wrestling with himself and with God.

Going a stone's throw away (Lk 22:41), Jesus began to be filled with fear and distress (Mk 14:34). No attempt is made to explain this. No blow had as yet fallen upon him, nor had he yet been scourged or crowned with thorns. Nevertheless, something strange was taking place, and the spectacle is somewhat unnerving. It was one thing to see the Master wet and cold, hungry and thirsty, fatigued or hot, but quite another to see him in a state of fright. It was unlike him to be anything but calm and self-possessed. Some find this side of Jesus reassuring proof of his humanity; others are repelled by the sight of a grown man grovelling with fear. In ancient times Celsus considered that Jesus displayed a contemptible weakness in the garden where he had gone trying to avoid arrest, instead of selling his life dearly, like a man. But there is more to it than this pagan could see.

There were two perfectly good reasons for Jesus' feelings in the garden. On a purely natural level, the threat of death causes fear. Nature provides us with an automatic reaction to anything that threatens our existence—a twisted arm, a push, a slight wound, even a harsh word brings about a reaction out of all proportion to the pain. This is because pain of any kind is a foretaste of our inevitable dissolution. Being truly human, Jesus was profoundly moved at the prospect of his own death. "With every desire to avoid unwarranted psychological interpretation," writes V. Taylor, "it is impossible to do any kind of justice to Mark's words without seeing in them something of the astonishment of the Son of Man who knows that he is also the Suffering Servant of Isaiah."

But there is more. The second and principal reason for Jesus' mental anguish was spiritual, not physical. No one has described these sufferings better than Cardinal Newman. Here is the opening paragraph of his marvellous sermon on the mental sufferings of Jesus in his passion.

> There then in that most awful hour, knelt the Savior of the world, putting off the defences of his divinity, dismissing his reluctant angels, who in myriads were ready at his call, and opening his arms, baring his breast sinless as he was, to the assault of the foe—of a foe whose breath was a pestilence, and whose embrace was an agony. There he knelt, motionless and still, while the vile and horrible fiend clad his spirit in a robe steeped in all that is hateful and heinous in human crime, which clung close round his heart and filled his conscience, and found its way into every sense and pore of his mind, and spread over him a moral leprosy, till he almost felt himself to be that which he never could be, and which his foe would fain have made him. (2 Cor 5:21.)

So sin now enters the picture, not Jesus' own, but the sins of all men. As the Suffering Servant, the man of suffering was "pierced for our offenses, crushed for our sins. Upon him was the chastisement that makes us whole, by his stripes we were healed" (Is 53:3–5). Jesus realized in the garden the enormity of the sins for which he was to give his life—an appalling price. In addition, he may well have been saddened at Peter's denials, at Judas' betrayal, at the failure of his mission to his own people.

In his anguish, Jesus turned to prayer. "He advanced a little and fell prostrate in prayer" (Mt 26:39; see Lk 22:41). His calm deserted him. Shaken to the depths of his being he fell prostrate to the ground. There are other positions for prayer. At the Wailing Wall (that is, a section of the southwest wall of the Temple area, put up when Herod the Great rebuilt the Jerusalem Temple, and left standing by the Romans when they took the city in 70 A.D.), Jewish men and women stand in prayer. Christians usually kneel when they pray.

Addressing his Father with great earnestness (Jerome uses the word *blandiens*, "beseeching" or even "wheedling" him), Jesus cried out, "My Father, if it is possible, let this cup pass me by. Still, let it be as you would have it, not as I" (Mt 26:39). Mark's "Abba, Father" is a combination of Aramaic and Greek, which may well be the original form. (It may also be a primitive liturgical bi-lingual prayer.) "Take this cup away from me" (Mk 14:36). The cup placed in front of one at table represented his share of the wine. As time went on, the word "cup" became a symbol of joy or of suffering, or it stood for a man's lot or destiny (Jn 18:11). It was frequently joined to divine wrath (see Ps 75:8 and Is 51:17), and something of this last applies here; Jesus was to drink the cup of divine wrath, that is, to suffer for everyman's sins. He struggled for some time with the idea in prayer but, appalling as the prospect was, his prayer was: "Let it be as you would have it, not as I."

Jesus and Prayer

Nowhere in the gospels is Jesus presented more vividly as a man of prayer than in the garden of Gethsemani. There is no sight more spectacular than that of a man at prayer, for prayer is something only man can do. The stars and the atoms of the cosmos are not free; they have no voices nor any choice but to do what they do. Man prays. His prayer is a contact of creature with creator, a dynamic communication of two minds. Man can praise God, or, by unfolding his own desires before him, ask that he fulfill them. Jesus was the perfect man of prayer.

When writing about great men, it is customary to stress their strong points and to soft-pedal their weaknesses. Customary or natural, the process can be overdone. One can so emphasize Jesus' relationship with his Father as to overlook his humanity, a fault of colossal proportions. Theology has done itself proud here by insisting upon the reality of Jesus' human nature. Strange as it may seem, this point has had to be defended, for there have been those who denied that Jesus ever had (1) a real body with human instincts and feelings, (2) a human soul endowed with (3) a human mind or intelligence and (4) a human will. If he had lacked any one of these he would not have been a truly human being. And if he had possessed all human abilities, yet was denied the chance to use them, he would have been nothing more than a robot. Mankind was not redeemed by robots which do not and cannot pray.

Prayer is an acknowledgement of human limitation, and the recognition of Another who holds the whole world in his hands, and who respects the free will of his creature, man. Many are the gifts of God, but there are many others to be given only if asked for. Divine providence allows for genuine secondary causes, and prayer—the expression of human desires—is such a cause. Jesus could and did pray.

The New Testament pictures Jesus as a man of activity and energy. Many times did he state his will: "Be clean." "Receive your sight!" With a confidence and composure wholly remarkable, he multiplied loaves and fishes, stilled wind and wave, summoned Lazarus to come forth from the tomb. None of these things are within the power of the naked human will, but Jesus' human will was the conjoined instrument of his divinity, in somewhat the same way that a human hand like that of Michelangelo can be the instrument of marvellous genius. But no mere human comparison can do justice to the harmony existing between Jesus' human will and that of his Father.

By a deliberate act of his human will, Jesus chose to drink of the cup of pain and suffering and death. Why did he do this? Such things are anything but desirable in themselves. Why did he not avoid them? Because he wished to be one with mankind, that is, because of sin, subject to pain and suffering and death. Thus did he take his place with sinners, and by his act of love and obedience he made atonement for all their sins, and reunited mankind with God. Such love and compassion escape our understanding, but not our gratitude. We grasp a little of the inner processes of Jesus' mind by looking upon suffering as a means to an end. In our world, we endure painful visits to hospitals and dentists in order to have better health. We do not wish pain; that would be contrary to all our instincts. But our real desire and will is to face it. Jesus did what had to be done to redeem his brothers and sisters.

In the garden of Gethsemani, Jesus deliberately embraced the suffering and death required of him in his role as Redeemer. His prayer, "Let this cup pass me by," reflected his aversion for the pain and humiliation and shame that awaited him. But at the same time he resolved to do what the Father wished: "Let it be as you would have it, not as I." His anguish and inner torment reveal to the world his genuine humanity, his prayer, his firm resolve.

In the history of spirituality there have been believers who entered deeply into the sufferings of Jesus. In an attempt to describe the experience, Mother Mary of Jesus wrote: "A *yes* arises from my heart, and at the same time my nature utters a great cry of horror." One could hardly better express the anguish felt by the Savior as he prayed in the garden.

The Apostles Sleep

So intimate is the union of soul and body that the one interacts upon the other. Our term "psychosomatic" refers to this. Inner anxieties communicate something to the body. The body reacts; some wring their hands, some pace the floor, some weep in an effort to find relief from inner struggles. The time was about midnight, or even later. Jesus rose from the ground and went back to the disciples. Left to themselves in the garden, after a long day and a long evening, they had fallen asleep. Charitable Luke ascribes their sleep to sorrow, which indeed does produce a heaviness of mind and body but also at times insomnia as well. Jesus' words at the Last Supper had been disturbing: he was to leave them, and to be betrayed by one of them. Peter had rejected the idea of his ever failing his master—"Though all may have their faith in you shaken, mine will never be shaken," he had said (Mt 26:33). The fiery sons of Zebedee had confidently asserted their ability to drink the cup Jesus was to drink (20:22). Brave words, and sincere, but none of them had been able to stay awake. Jesus awakened them, saying, "So you could not stay awake with me for even an hour?" Peter's honesty compelled him later on to record this incident, so little to his credit. "Be on guard," Jesus went on, "and pray that you may not undergo the test." Harsh reality did indeed lie ahead, and the words were a timely reminder of it. But even the most resolute man has to reckon with the flesh. "The spirit is willing, but nature is weak." Jesus knew what was in a man.

Finding no support from his friends, Jesus again sought relief in prayer. He faced the inevitable reality—ahead lay suffering and pain, but "if this cannot pass me by without my drinking it, your will, My Father, be done." The die was cast. A second and a third time he went back to his disciples, only to find them sleeping. "Sleep on now and enjoy your rest" (Mt), he said, or as Mk puts it: "Still sleeping? Still taking your ease? It will have to do." Mark's questions seem to fit better than Matthew's plain statement; the questions become expressions of Jesus' pain and disappointment. Mark's phrase "It will have to do" may also be rendered "It is all over." At Gethsemani a real battle had been fought and won. Jesus did not then and there drain the painful cup, but then and there he consented to drink it. All was now ready for the next stage in the struggle for the salvation of God's sinful creature, man.

The Angel of Gethsemani

After his fast and temptation in the desert, angels had come to minister unto Jesus. Now in the garden, another angel appears to him. The Greek verb used here (*ophthe*) suggests that it was a visible apparition. Some have held that the devil had returned, for after tempting Jesus in the desert, he had "left him . . . for a while" (Lk 4:13). But this runs contrary to the text which states that the angel was from heaven and had come to strengthen him. Could Luke have made the angel a symbol of Jesus' victory over his fears? Actually Luke made little of Jesus' fear up to this point. Others have identified the angel with Mary of Bethany, who had come looking for Jesus and, seen amid the shadows and moonlight, was mistaken for an angel. Truly, it is easier to believe Luke meant a real angel.

An angel then appeared to him from heaven, to strengthen him (Lk 22:43). Jesus' sufferings had already begun, and they were inward sufferings. Thus the angel's comforting must have been directed to Jesus' spirit. "*How*," Lagrange remarks dryly, "is God's secret." Aquinas perceived in the angel a proof of Jesus' genuine humanity. In moments of trial, the physical presence of friends becomes a source of strength. One senses that he is not alone. At wakes, for example, friends are a comfort both by just being there, and also because they say things about the deceased which the bereaved one knows even better than they—"he was a good man, she a good woman." Such words, gratefully listened to, temper the sorrow of bereavement. The root meaning of our word "comfort" is to be brave *along with* someone. Comforting is a kind of strengthening.

But how could the angel comfort and strengthen the God-Man? Could the angel tell him anything he did not already know? Perhaps not, but he could review these things with him. Did not Moses and Elijah converse with him about his coming passion and death? Could not the angel have spoken about the splendid effects of the passion? Dying would not be conquered, but death would be, and both suffering and death would be ennobled and given new meaning. Sufferings like those of Jesus, or those endured in union with him, are symbolic of love and obedience. Jesus willingly became the expiatory victim for our sins. "For our sakes" as Paul writes, "God made him who did not know sin, to be sin, so that in him we might become the very holiness of God" (2 Cor 5:21). Once the world had seen divine love in bodily form embracing suffering and death out of love and obedience, it would never be the same again, and future ages would bring forth heroic souls who would reflect some of that love upon the world.

Surely the man Jesus would not have been unmoved by such ideas.

The Bloody Sweat

Only in Luke is it recorded that "Jesus in his anguish prayed with all the greater intensity" (22:44). The word here translated as "anguish" is, in Greek, the word "agony." Originally that word described the supreme effort of an athlete to win the crown. In our times, the word is usually associated with one's last gasp, or the death-agony. What Luke had in mind was the wider meaning of a moment of severe crisis or struggle. In the garden, Jesus' victory over sin by way of the cross hung in the balance with his human reluctance to suffer. Jesus met the crisis in a highly instructive way—"he prayed with all the greater intensity." He did something more than that: "His sweat became like drops of blood falling to the ground."

History records instances of a red or bloody sweat which is called "haematidrosis." Explanations are difficult, but always involve stressful situations. Sudden fright drains blood from the face and causes one to grow pale, while anger brings blood rushing to the face. Possibly the two can be combined here. If Jesus' original fright had been severe, his reaction to it may have been correspondingly strong. (Narrow escapes from death have been followed by violent anger.) At first dismayed at the cost of his death, Jesus forcefully resolved to go through with it. And then his blood came oozing through his skin. This sweat was possibly restricted to his brow and face, where perspiration is most noticeable. In any case, we are not here dealing with something pleasant; even a bloody rash causes intense irritation. And more is involved here than a mere physiological movement of the blood. The text says plainly enough that Jesus at prayer was in great anguish of mind as well as of body.

The two verses of Luke which describe Jesus' agony and bloody sweat are missing from many ancient and important manuscripts (A, B, N, R, T, W), from some cursives (13,69) and some of the versions, but are found in Sinaiticus, D, Koridethi, in other cursives, in the Old Latin, and many of the versions. The verses are certainly authentic, that is, canonical and inspired, as the Council of Trent has declared. Their omission can be more easily understood than their addition. Theological scruples, and the fear lest the Arians might make use of this text to deny Jesus' divinity, may have led to their omission in some manuscripts.

Among the ancients, Euthymius alone held that Luke intended only to say that Jesus sweated profusely. In that case, however, there was no reason for him to have said "like drops of blood falling to the ground." Our expression, "to sweat blood" probably derives from the gospel account, a graphic metaphor to express a truly anxious moment.

Whatever the nature of this phenomenon, it signified an extreme anguish of mind that must have reduced Jesus to a state of near exhaustion. Here his human nature appears in all its capacity to suffer. But how eloquently it speaks of Jesus' great love for man.

The Sufferings of Jesus

Familiar throughout their long history with persecution and hardship, the Chosen People looked upon suffering without enthusiasm. They were not alone in this. In the pagan world dominated by Spartan code and Stoic rules of conduct, admiration was reserved for bravery, strength, and success. The real man faced the world fearlessly, and never gave his enemy the satisfaction of knowing that he had inflicted a hurt. The model Stoic never acknowledged pain. There is the ancient story about a boy who, finding a half-frozen fox, placed the animal inside his tunic. As the lad stood talking to his father the animal revived and tore at his benefactor's heart. The youth betrayed no awareness of the pain until he dropped lifeless at his father's feet.

It was to people molded by this pagan outlook and the human aversion to pain that the story of the God-Man had to be preached. Those who first heard the story of Jesus' death on a cross found it ridiculous. A Savior who willingly assumed the responsibility for the crimes of all mankind? Who could give him a second thought? He must have been some sort of fool, and certainly less than a red-blooded man.

At the same time, everyone will admit that there are times when a refusal to admit pain or sadness betrays a lack of common sense. Not to fear when one ought to reveals an abnormal insensitivity. A real man knows what is happening to him. A brave man faced with suffering and pain will not come apart at the seams but will acknowledge them, confront them, and if need be, endure them. Jesus was determined to drink the cup of his passion to show his solidarity with the human race, and to give a supreme example of his love for his heavenly Father and for his brothers. Jesus was no Stoic, but on the other hand he was no coward either. He showed himself to be like ourselves, and we can relate to such a Savior who was no stranger to suffering and death.

In the face of suffering, Jesus seems to come off a poor second to certain of the martyrs who endured their torments without any indication of pain or suffering. St. Lawrence is remembered as the martyr who, while being roasted alive, informed his executioners that they could "turn him over" as he was "done on one side." Another saint was obliged to walk over live coals; they seemed to him like a soft carpet of rose petals. Closer to our times, St. Thomas More smilingly asked his executioner to disengage his beard ("it has committed no treason") from the block.

Humanly speaking, there is some explanation of all this. In the heat of battle the adrenalin flows and soldiers or athletes seem unaware of blows received; they simply disregard them. In other cases, the realization by some martyrs that they were suffering for their beloved Master and thus bearing witness to him, filled them with an intense spiritual joy, which in great measure cancelled out their perception of their pains.

In Jesus' case, such an overflow of spirit upon body was simply not permitted. His pain was pure and unadulterated, and immense in extent. And along with it, he had an uninterrupted and loving communion with his Father.

Jesus and Human Suffering

Some spiritual writers have indulged in extravagant exaggerations, comparing Jesus' sufferings with those of the souls in Purgatory. But the comparison not only limps, it is illicit from the beginning, for the certain reason that this life and the next are so different that they cannot be linked together for comparison. Nor should one compare the sufferings of the Savior with those of the damned. However striking it might be to suppose that Jesus' great love for man was so great that he momentarily set aside the vision of God's face so as to be able to suffer the pains of the damned, theology will have none of this. Two things are wrong with such an opinion. First, there is nothing redemptive in the pains suffered by the damned, and secondly, the Beatific Vision is not something that can be turned on or off at will. If it has one glimpse of the Supreme Good wherein are contained all the perfections and beauty which created things only faintly reflect, the blessed soul will never look away again. Not that in heaven one loses his freedom; rather, the soul willingly and lovingly gazes upon the infinitely perfect, unchanging God. Aside from him there is nothing that can attract the soul. Jesus could never for a moment tear his gaze from the face of his Father.

Jesus sufferings have also been compared to those of the mystics. Mysticism is a difficult word. In the popular mind, a mystic is a man or woman who is slightly out of touch with reality, and who pursues some shadowy objective that is really not all that important. Such an evaluation of mystics or of mysticism is unfortunate. The term seems derived from the Greek word *muo*, which means "to close one's mouth, to be quiet." Mystics therefore are those who zealously cultivate an attitude of rapt attention to a God who is ever-present in the world, and more real to them than reality itself. As for their being out of touch with real life, the great mystics were great saints very much involved with real life. Far from being withdrawn from humankind, they were generally wholesome people, forgetful of self and given to heroic service of their fellow men and women.

In addition to their intense interior life, the mystics were invariably men and women terribly familiar with suffering. As these spiritual giants drew near to the summit of perfection, their sufferings intensified. They had already acquired solid virtue and had gone through the purification of the senses; there remained the purification of the soul, a mysterious state characterized by darkness, but a prelude to a sublime union with God. Three great Carmelites—Teresa of Avila, John of the Cross, and Therese of Lisieux—tried to explain in their writings what was going on in their souls at this moment. Many do not find these attempts notably successful, since they use such paradoxical phrases as a martyrdom of pain and delight, of delicious burnings, of inebriating wounds. They experienced intense suffering along with a profound inner peace. The Little Flower said that what she experienced was not merely a darkness nor a wall that caused darkness; *this* darkness blotted out the stars. But she, like all the saints, absorbed suffering and radiated love, somewhat as a plant absorbs carbon dioxide and gives off oxygen into the air.

It is wrong to compare Jesus' sufferings with those of the mystics. Their sufferings were part of a process that purified their faith and their confidence or trust in God. Jesus was blessed with the Beatific Vision from the moment of his conception, and so had knowledge rather than faith. Nor did he hope in God as some future reward; he saw God and possessed him already. Yet neither the vision, nor his actual possession of God in this life, meant that Jesus was spared suffering. He was utterly unique in that in him—a divine person incarnate—there were two natures. There was no osmosis, no spillover from one to the other. The two natures were there almost as if each was there alone. Jesus therefore could suffer in his human nature. Like ours, his sufferings were real.

Our religion contains many profound mysteries. It is the function of theology to safeguard mystery, not to explain it. One should beware of seemingly intelligible explanations of divine mysteries. It is not an exaggeration to say that the clearest explanations of those divine mysteries often fail to do justice to them.

After some time in prayer and suffering, Jesus rejoined his disciples. "Rouse yourselves and come along," he said. "See, my betrayer is at hand" (Mk 14:42). The messianic ministry enters upon its climax. "The Son of Man is about to be handed over to the power of evil men." The decisive battle had been won in the garden during Jesus' prayer. Now he is calm, ready for what lies ahead. His serenity and self-possession were, under the circumstances, a remarkable illustration of his character, and of the power of prayer.

CHAPTER FIVE

Judas Iscariot

Who Was Judas Iscariot?

Jude, Judah, and Judas are all forms of the one name. Although its etymology is uncertain, the name may mean "May the Lord be praised." It is an honorable name, then, and one borne proudly by many great men. Judah was the fourth son of the patriarch Jacob. The tribe of Judah, which eventually was to stand for the entire people, was named after him. From this tribe arose many famous kings (like David and Solomon), prophets (like Isaiah and Jeremiah) and military leaders (Judas Maccabeus). There was an ancient prophecy about Judah:

> The sceptre shall never depart from Judah nor the ruler's staff from between his feet, until he comes to whom it belongs; and to him shall be the obedience of the peoples (Gn 49:10).

These lines have traditionally been understood in a messianic way. The passage certainly foretells the supremacy of the tribe of Judah which found its fulfillment in the Davidic dynasty and ultimately in Jesus Christ, the son of David. When Jerusalem fell to the Babylonians its proud inhabitants were carried off into an exile that lasted for half a century (587–538 B.C.). Only a remnant was to return to the homeland and to represent the whole of the nation.

Judas Iscariot is the tragic figure of the New Testament, a

complex and difficult personality. He came from a village called Qarioth (*Ish-cariot* means "man from Qarioth"), variously identified with a Qarioth south of Hebron or with Abu Gosh west of Jerusalem. This geographic fact is not without interest, for all the other apostles came from Galilee. Judas came from the harsh, upland province of Judah. (One author, H.V. Morton, compares Judea to a tawny tiger, crouched and ready to spring.) Judas was possibly more intelligent and better educated than the Eleven. He had, as we might put it, drive and push. There was an abortive move to make Jesus king after he had multiplied the loaves (Jn 6:15). The next day, something prompted Jesus to ask his disciples, "Do you want to leave me too? (6:60–67). Was Judas behind the agitation? There is also the fact that when Mary anointed Jesus' feet with expensive ointment (12:1–7), Judas was shocked at the "waste," and cried out "Why was not this perfume sold? It could have brought 300 pieces of silver, and the money have been given to the poor." Judas cleverly masked his irritation by referring to Jesus' known solicitude for the poor. Indeed, Judas had been entrusted with the management of the group's money. John the evangelist bluntly states that Judas was a thief, and was known to have helped himself to money from the common purse. These harsh words find an echo in other places in the gospel where the apostles are listed by name. Peter is always first to be mentioned, and Judas the last. Attached to Judas' name is the word "traitor." (See Jn 6:70, and Mt 10:2.)

Why Judas Betrayed Jesus

One of the great problems of the New Testament is why Judas betrayed his Master. Some have denied that he did, as there was no need for him to do so; Jesus' arrest was only a matter of time. But it is extremely unlikely that anyone would have invented so sordid a story. Judas is a real person, a flesh and blood figure, not just a fleshing-out of texts from the psalms (41:9 and 55:12f for example). As a prime example of baseness, he had been relegated in the popular mind to hell (see Dante, *Inferno* 23:61f), and his name is now synonymous with treachery. Various attempts have been made to white-wash Judas, but not many are conviced by them. Here are some of these attempts.

Judas Was the Savior of the Law of Moses. According to some authors, Judas, like everyone else, was at first taken in by Jesus of Nazareth. However, he was much smarter than his companions, and it gradually dawned on him that this so-called Messiah was heading in a dangerous direction. Jesus seemed quite unconcerned with the sacred Sabbath, and frequently ignored the Sabbath rest. He set himself up as an interpreter of the Law, and his "but I say to you" indicated that he thought himself to be greater than Moses. Besides, he was critical of the custodians and interpreters of the Law. Worse still, he preached an odd kind of humility, failed to capitalize on several excellent opportunities to have himself proclaimed king, and urged payment of taxes to Caesar. Judas wanted a strong, vigorous Messiah, and initially had thought Jesus was that man. Now he began to suspect the worst, that Jesus was a pseudo-Messiah, and, while perhaps not a bad man personally, was by that very fact all the more dangerous. If allowed to go on unchecked, he could destroy the law of Moses.

The turmoil in Judas' mind grew. How could he possibly and in good conscience remain loyal to such a teacher? God had spoken face to face on Mount Sinai with his friend Moses. A man would be a fool not to side with Moses. Judas may have remembered a text from Deuteronomy (13:2–6) which sounded a warning about the appearance of false prophets, and gave instructions how to deal with them. "That prophet or dreamer shall be put to death . . . thus shall you purge the evil from your midst." Judas found himself in a painful dilemma whether to remain loyal to Jesus or to the Law. He made up his mind. By delivering Jesus into the hands of the Sanhedrin, he would become the savior of the Mosaic Law, and of his own good name. A euphoric peace of mind descended upon him.

But why did not Judas simply sever his ties with Jesus? That he accepted money for the betrayal of a friend tells us a lot about the real Judas. He was no lofty savior of the Law, but a morally unattractive person. Instead of just walking no more with Jesus, he committed a base act. He has never been a hero, not even to his own people.

Judas Was a Messianic Instigator. In Renan's *Life of Jesus,* Judas figures in an ingenious theory which still finds an occasional supporter. Judas was well-meaning. Perceiving that the Sanhedrin had resolved to bring about Jesus' death, he decided to take the initiative and force the issue, knowing all the while that it would all come out all right. Was not Jesus the long-awaited Messiah? To hasten the moment of his triumph, all Judas had to do was to steer him into a situation where he would have to exercise his divine power. The people had shown they wanted to make him a king; if it came to a show of force, the people would rise up and save him. The scheme could not miss, and the messianic kingdom would then become a fact. Was Judas not a friend of Jesus? Did he not kiss Jesus in the garden? And had not Jesus himself approved the plan when he said to him at the Last Supper, "Be quick about what you are to do" (Jn 13:27).

Unfortunately, the plan backfired. Jesus was arrested, the people turned against him, and he was led off to a certain death. Judas was stricken with remorse, and he took his own life in a futile gesture of reparation for what he had done.

This reconstruction of facts conficts radically with the gospel. Judas is not portrayed as a messianic instigator, but as a traitor who bargained away the life of a friend. The gospels never fail to refer to him as "the one who betrayed" his master. Peter would deny his Master out of fear, yet Jesus risen from the dead sent word to pardon him especially (Mk 16:7). Peter was forgiven because of his repentance. Not Judas.

A Greedy, Disillusioned Man. It is far more likely that Judas' love for money was mixed with other passions that led him to his betrayal. Few men are traitors for money alone; prospects of gain are not always the main motive. There can be a desire for revenge, a chip on one's shoulder, a tinge of madness or misdirected idealism, or any combination of these. In Judas' case, his greed may have been accompanied by some shattered dream, a failed ambition.

In the beginning, like many others, Judas considered Jesus to be the long-awaited and soon-to-be-glorious king of Israel (Jn 1:49, 6:15; Lk 19:11, 24:21; Acts 1:5). In fact, in the early days of his public ministry, Jesus did manifest signs of power, signs which could have served to feed the fiery ambitions of the unscrupulous. Judas was already an important man in the Twelve, and it is not hard to imagine him dreaming about the role he would one day play in the kingdom the Wonder-Worker would set up. Enchanting thoughts, but soon disturbed by others. Jesus made no attempt to mobilize the crowds of enthusiastic listeners for a take-over of power. The "job-description" of his followers was not particularly appealing; the cost of discipleship was in fact peculiar: "Follow me, bear your cross daily, give up what you have . . . Blessed are the poor" (indeed!). "Learn of me who am meek and humble of heart" (insanity!).

The climax came when Mary anointed Jesus' feet with such lavish prodigality. Judas protested the waste, estimating the ointment at 300 denarii (Mt 26:9; Mk 14:4f; Jn 12:3). Then, when Jesus calmly predicted his coming death, Judas knew that it was all over; he had been backing the wrong man, a man now calmly going to his death. Judas then realized that his own future had suddenly become precarious. Once Jesus had been put out of the way, his enemies would look for his associates and friends. And when they came they would find Judas—an important man among the Twelve. He was, he realized, himself a marked man.

At this juncture, Judas' calculating nature asserted itself. He resolved both to save his own skin and become a bit richer in the bargain. He had only to facilitate Jesus' arrest—which was already only a matter of time—and he would be cleansed of the stigma of having been his friend and apostle.

Mark relates (14:1f) that the chief priests and scribes were seeking Jesus' death, and that Judas presented himself to them with a plan. His crude question "How much is it worth to you?" must have brought a cynical smile to their lips; so money talked even to the followers of the unworldly Galilean!

A paltry sum, thirty silver pieces, was counted into Judas' hands. They made a pleasing sound as they fell.

Men often do not see beyond their noses; dark deeds look dark in the light of day. At some moment—perhaps when he saw Jesus being marched off from the Sanhedrin to Pilate— Judas was struck by what he had done. He hastened to the chief priests and offered them back the money. "I did wrong to deliver up an innocent man" (Mt 27:4). Too late. They contemptuously dismissed him. He cast the money away. It flashed through the air, rang noisily upon the stones. Without a backward look, Judas turned and disappeared.

Judas' Death

Judas' death is recorded twice. Matthew stresses the fact of his crime and subsequent despair. Luke (Acts 1:16–19) views his death as punishment for his crime. It is difficult to disentangle the details. The field where Judas died was purchased by the chief priests and was known as the Field of Blood (Haceldama) because it had been purchased with Jesus' blood-money. In Luke's account, the blood was Judas'. He purchased the field, and there he fell down and burst asunder. It is not clear just when or how Judas died; Matthew says it was by hanging. Luke and Matthew appeal to different scripture passages: Luke to Psalm 69:26; 109:8; Matthew to Zech 11:12f. The free quotation from Zechariah is combined with Jer 32:6–15 (the purchase of a field; cf. 18:2; 19:1). In conclusion, Matthew and Acts are agreed as to the essentials: Judas' death, his motive and the place.

How did Judas differ from the other apostles? Peter the rock talked a lot, and at a crucial moment, ran for his life. James and John were called sons of thunder, and were ready to summon fire from heaven upon the rude Samaritans who refused them hospitality. Thomas obstinately refused to take anyone's word for things. Judas was not the only apostle with failings.

Judas failed to repent for what he had done. Peter shed tears when Jesus looked at him; Judas shed no tears but conceded that he had "done wrong." He could have openly aligned himself with his captive master. Beyond question he should have asked the Father's forgiveness for what he had done. Instead he committed the ultimate sin, and, despairing of God's goodness and mercy, took his own life (Mt 27:4f). Origen here remarks that the devil may at times allow a man a brief respite, but only with the view of plunging him more deeply into sin.

What can be said of Jesus' choice of Judas as an apostle? Was he truly a "knower of hearts"? Did he not know what was in a man (Acts 1:24; 15:8)? Could he not have foreseen that Judas would betray him? Yes, but like his heavenly Father, Jesus was a great respecter of human freedom. Judas did not have to do what he did. God bestows great graces, Lagrange remarks, even upon those who will one day fail him.

St. John Chrysostom once posed this uncomfortable question: "And you, dear reader, do you never betray Christ?" We might well ask, "Is it I, Lord?"

The Fate of Judas

The New Testament says nothing of Judas' ultimate fate. Some Bible readers find themselves wondering if Judas is in heaven or in hell. Did not Jesus say, speaking of the one who was to betray the Son of Man: "Woe to that man by whom the Son of Man is betrayed. It would have been better for that man if he had not been born!" (Mt 26:24)? Again, at the Last Supper, as he addressed his Father in prayer, he recalled that he had lost none of those whom the Father had entrusted to him except—"the son of perdition" (Jn 17:12). These are harsh words from the Good Shepherd.

The Church assures us that there is a hell, but has never declared that there was anyone in it. On the other hand, the Church has never made a saint out of Judas. The problem of Judas' fate is insoluble but interesting, for it affords exegetes and theologians an opportunity to explore the teachings of the faith. Let us see what can be said.

"*Woe* to that man . . ." is an expression at least of disappointment or grief over the undefined but unpleasant future that Judas had brought upon himself. In this sense, the word is sometimes rendered as "Alas!" The context itself seems to demand a certain harshness, according to Jerome, who thought that a man undeterred by shame from doing evil, might be brought to his senses by the promise of punishment. (Jesus spoke these words at the Last Supper while Judas was present.) Better for that man not to be at all, than to be badly.

We are wrestling here with a biblical paradox. Jesus' betrayal was the fulfillment of scripture (Ps 41:9; 55:13), yet Judas is blamed for what he deliberately chose to do. Could he have done otherwise? Of course. All men are born with the tremendous power to choose between good and evil. The fact that Jesus' death was in God's plan does not mean that God approves of betrayal. God is so powerful that he can bring good out of evil (which he tolerates, but does not cause). That however does not make a bad act good. To the contrary, there is an objective standard. Right is right even if nobody acts rightly; wrong is wrong even if everybody is wrong.

Jesus' words, "woe to that man . . . , " were not for Judas' ears alone. Across the ages, those words have set in motion many a salutary examination of conscience.

When it comes his turn to speak, the theologian states clearly that God creates no one in order to condemn him. However, one can choose to go to hell if he persists in a sinful choice of something seriously sinful. One takes his history with him into the next life. Life on earth is a succession of fleeting moments. Death spells an end to time, which becomes, as it were, an endless *now*. If one enters eternity with a will fixed on sin, if there has been no yielding to God's will and no repentence even in the last split-second of time, then one can choose hell. No need to place locks on the doors of hell. None of hell's inhabitants want to leave.

Some theologians periodically argue that hell is an affront to God's goodness and mercy. It is argued that God takes into consideration a man's genes, his background, education and external circumstances, and that in his mercy he pardons all sinners, with a generosity and understanding suitable to a good God. Attractive? Yes, in a way, but the question is whether this proposition is good theology.

First, we should note that the fact that a position has been challenged and attacked does not mean that this position is necessarily weak and indefensible, or that one should abandon it. The Bible consistently speaks of sin as something that arouses divine resentment. God makes clear promises, but makes clear demands as well. The first of his demands is that he alone be acknowledged as God. Sin is open defiance, which God will not tolerate from his creature. The man who sins incurs guilt, and also the obligation to repent and make reparation for sin. This makes sense, for if both evil and good are ultimately to be rewarded with unending bliss, all morality becomes meaningless. Indeed, this makes Jesus' death upon the cross unnecessary and meaningless. All men instinctively know that there is a good to do and an evil to avoid.

God has two arms, so to speak—mercy and justice. Like God himself, who *is* whatever can be attributed to him, his mercy and justice are infinite, to be found wherever God is. St. Thomas saw the divine mercy at work in all of God's works, even in hell where sinners were punished, but not as harshly as strict justice would have demanded. It has been argued that by bringing all men to heaven, God would be showing that his mercy rewards sinners more than his justice requires their punishment. But that would make a travesty of justice. Man's redemption did not come cheaply. We were purchased at great cost.

One last consideration. Would it be an act of divine mercy to annihilate the sinner, rather than to shut him up in a state of eternal torment? There is no trace of this solution in scripture, and theologians are quick to point out that it is not a good one. God is also infinitely wise, and he does not take back gifts once given (Rom 11:29). He can never undo anything that he has in his infinite wisdom acomplished. He created man in his own image, endowed him with a spiritual nature, destined to unending life. He cannot, without ceasing to be God, undo his creation.

In conclusion: If Judas died unrepentent and despairing, then he must be and should be in hell. If he repented, he could be in heaven. Since scripture is silent on both counts, we cannot assign him his final place. Could he possibly be held in a place of purification until the end of time? Of this, scripture says nothing, nor does the Church. We had best leave Judas in God's hands, and be ourselves careful not to offend God by our own sins. For we, like Judas, must pay for our sins.

CHAPTER SIX

The Arrest

The gospel account of Judas' actions and of Christ's actual arrest is remarkable for its compactness and brevity. No attempt is made to explain why Judas acted as he did, and the actual scene of betrayal is delineated with a master's touch. Not all is clear, but it is clear enough.

The night of the Passover was to be spent in Jerusalem (Dt 16:17), so Judas was fairly certain where he would be able to find Jesus (Jn 18:2). The garden of Gethsemani was a short distance from the Temple and could be considered part of the city. It easily lay within the limits of movement allowed by the feast day.

Judas approached the garden in the company of three groups of people who ordinarily did not consort with one another: the Temple police sent by the chief priests and scribes and elders, the servants of the highpriest, and lastly, Romans from the military garrison in Jerusalem. The presence of Roman soldiers at this stage of the proceedings is surprising. How they came to be involved is not clear. John speaks of a cohort of soldiers. A cohort was a tenth of a legion, or 600 men, far more than necessary for the night's work. The word may refer to a much smaller unit. Matthew and Mark both speak of a crowd armed with swords and clubs, a crowd's usual weapons.

While Jesus was speaking to his disciples, Judas arrived with this small posse. They carried lamps and torches in case their quarry tried to hide in the shadows of the garden. As things turned out, there was no need for lights. Seizing the initiative, Jesus suddenly appeared before them at the edge of the garden. They had not expected this, and his calm question "Who is it you want?" was disconcerting. Eventually someone replied that they were seeking "Jesus the Nazorean" (the name by which Jesus was known to his contemporaries). With these words the passion formally begins. Jesus replied simply, "I am he," and those who had come to arrest him "retreated slightly and fell to the ground" (Jn 18:6). This might be one way of saying that the soldiers instinctively assumed a fighting crouch when they found their man before them. But John's account seems rather to indicate some exercise of superhuman powers on Jesus' part. John does not give the details of the betrayal, but instead emphasizes the fact that Jesus suffered because he willed to do so.

Judas approached Jesus and said, 'Peace, Rabbi," and kissed him. A kiss was indeed a clever way to identify the man who was to be arrested. Pointing could have been misleading; those who did not know Jesus by sight might have arrested the wrong man. But there would be no mistake. Judas was close enough to make sure of that. His kiss, to judge from the verb form (the imperfect), was "held" long enough to insure a positive identification.

It is difficult to do justice to Jesus' words here. Literally, they mean, "Friend, for what you have come." There is nothing in the words to suggest that they were uttered in a broken voice, or expressed an overwhelming sorrow. They are in fact so compressed that they are almost unintelligible. There is no problem with "friend" (*hetaire* in Greek), which means friend, comrade, companion, pupil. (Socrates' pupils were called *hetaire's*.) But "for what you have come" is so elliptical that one has to add "I know" ("I know why you are here"), or "Do . . ." ("Do what you came to do"). The latter addition would then appear to mean "that's enough of that," cutting short Judas' hypocritical kiss.

Peter stood close by, taking in the scene. It was difficult to grasp what was going on, but all became clear when Malchus, the highpriest's servant, moved toward the Master with rope or chain in his hand. Peter exploded into action. He whipped out his sword and struck at the advancing servant. Malchus dodged instinctively, but the sword sliced off his right ear (John, and Luke the physician note *which* ear it was). Jesus intervened at once: "Let (things) go on" or "Stop, no more of that!" Telling Peter to put his sword away, Jesus exercised his healing power, and touching the servant's ear, restored it. Jesus' love for peace cancelled out Peter's action, thus assuring his disciples' safety. Peter acted on impulse, but the edge of a sword is not the answer to all problems. The cross, not the sword, was to be the instrument of salvation. Jesus would not call legions of angels into action. He said, "Am I not to drink the cup the Father has given me?" (Jn 18:11). One hears the echo here of his prayer in the garden a few moments or hours ago.

Since the Father willed that his Son should suffer, Jesus would do so gladly. However, that Son reacted to his arrest in a very human way, for he sharply protested the way the whole business was being carried out. "Am I criminal that you come out after me armed with swords and clubs? When I was with you day after day in the temple you did not lay hands on me" (Lk 22:52–53). The scene was sordid and unnecessary. Then Jesus' amazement turned to resignation, "but this is your hour; this is the reign of darkness."

Mark's account of Jesus' arrest reflects something of the confusion of that night: the surprise, the threatening strangers who suddenly appear, the lateness of the hour, the confusion of the apostles. Mark also depicts Jesus as in control of both the scene and the hour. Isaiah's prophecy was being fulfilled: He surrendered himself to death, and was counted among the wicked (53:12). At this, "all of the disciples deserted him and fled" (Mk 14:50). Had they been pushed roughly about? They may have reasoned that Jesus could manage without them. Jesus remained, alone.

At this point, Mark records a curious incident (15:51–52). It is wholly irrelevant to the main story and has always been intriguing. A young man, apparently one known to the evangelist, followed Jesus that night, whether out of sympathy or curiosity or loyalty is not clear. The young man wore only a linen cloth wrapped about him. Poor people usually slept with their clothes on; that this man was naked under the sheet might indicate that he was from a well-to-do family. Next, for reasons that are not clear, the soldiers tried to seize him, but he slipped from the sheet and fled naked into the night. There the story ends.

Who was the young man? Surely not a disciple, for they were with Jesus and fully clothed. Moreover, they too were running away. Nor was he an inhabitant of the house in which the Last Supper had been eaten; Gethsemani was too far from it for anyone to venture from it wearing only a linen cloth. One might not unreasonably suppose that the young man lived somewhere near the garden. Hearing the commotion there he had come to see what was going on. Perhaps the man was Mark himself, who later put himself into the picture in much the same way that medieval artists used to paint themselves into the shadows or in a corner of their pictures. There is no unanimous opinion as to the identification of Mark's young man. The night has hidden him well.

CHAPTER SEVEN

The Trial

The trial of Jesus raises many difficult problems. Some of these are: the time and place of the Jewish trials, whether it was before the whole Sanhedrin or a few members, whether it was in the house of Annas or Caiaphas, whether there were two sessions or only one. Were all the legalities observed? How are the synoptics to be reconciled with John, who places the scourging before the outrages and mockery while the synopitcs have it the other way around. There is an argument about the place of the Roman trial. Some locate it in the Antonia, others in Herod's palace on the west side of the city. There is also a question about the size of the crowd, and its demand for an amnesty. Finally, who was responsible for Jesus' death? Are the gospels anti-Semitic, or unhistorical?

The Jewish Trial

Jesus was tried before the Sanhedrin, a body of elders who sat as a sort of Supreme Court. It consisted of elders from lay upperclass families, scribes, and priestly houses. In short, it was an aristocratic body. It sat in a special building called the Beth Din or "house of judgment." Also called *liskath haggazit*, this building was near the southwest corner of the Temple enclosure. Nothing of course now remains of any of these buildings or of the nearby stadium where Jewish youths diligently pursued Greek games.

The jurisdiction of the Sanhedrin was severely limited by both Herod the Great and by the Romans. However, it did enjoy great prestige and it had some real authority. Its letters of recommendation were honored as far away as Damascus (see Acts 9:2. Saul carried such letters). The Sanhedrin had the last word in matters relevant to the Mosaic Law. It also exercised some criminal jurisdiction. For example, it could have a man flogged, as Paul was in 2 Cor 11:24, but it did not have the right, the *jus gladii* or "the right of the sword," to impose the death penalty.

Since the gospels pass over the legal aspects of Jesus' trial, one must search elsewhere for the details of the procedure. There is a treatise found in the *Mishnah* which does provide these details. But caution is necessary. The Mishnah, a subdivision of the Talmud, was not committed to writing until the third century A.D. It seems clear that a body of Jewish law existed before the treatise, but it is not certain that these laws were anything more than theory at the time of Jesus. Indeed, if one were to look at Jesus' trial according to the Mishnah, there were many irregularities:

1.   The Sanhedrin was supposed to meet during the day, not at night (Acts 4:3). It was to hold its sessions in the *Beth Din* or Bouleterion.

2.   In plenary session, the greater Sanhedrin was to number seventy men, not counting the highpriest who presided (Ex 24:1,9; Nm 11:16). At least twenty-three of the seventy judges were obliged to be present in cases involving capital punishment.

3.   Cases that were punishable by death were to be treated in two sessions held on successive days. The first was for the trial, the second for the sentence. The first session could not be held on the eve of a festival day or the eve of the Sabbath.

4.   The testimony of conflicting witnesses was to be rejected.

5.   No judge was allowed to act as a witness in cases over which he was presiding.

6.   The voting was to begin with the youngest judge not the oldest, lest the prestige of the senior members influence the decision of the younger man. The highpriest presiding over the trial was never to begin the voting.

Jesus Before the Highpriests

Jesus was first brought to Annas (Jn 18:13), one of the most remarkable figures in Jewish history. Annas held the office of highpriest from A.D. 7-14, when he was deposed by the Roman procurator, Valerius Gratus. He was succeeded in office by his son Eleazar, by his son-in-law Joseph Caiaphas (A.D. 18-36), and by four other sons (up to A.D. 62). The Talmud has harsh things to say about Annas and his family and its "serpent-hissings," possibly referring to a family penchant for intrigue, bribery, avarice, and exploitation of the Temple monopoly on sacrificial offerings.

Annas did not release Christ from his bonds nor is it recorded that he even deigned to speak to the prisoner. He sent him on to Caiaphas. He may have wondered as he did so whether this poor specimen could truly be the man who had violently attacked the Scribes and Pharisees (Mt 23).

It was probably a very busy but a thoughtful and clever Caiaphas who had given the order to bring Christ first of all to Annas, his all-powerful father-in-law. Annas must have found the gesture pleasing. Annas and Caiaphas probably lived in adjoining wings of a large family compound; a tradition locates it near the Cenacle. It is not likely that the whole Sanhedrin (Mk 14:53) had assembled there at this tardy hour. Mark is probably in part anticipating the later morning session (see Luke), when he describes an emergency (night) session, attended in Caiaphas' house by members of the Sanhedrin known to be hostile to Jesus.

The highpriest and his colleagues questioned Jesus about his disciples and his teaching; Jesus focused attention upon himself; his "I" is emphatic. His doctrine was no conspiracy. "I have spoken openly to the world. I have always taught in synagogues and in the temple [area] where all Jews come together. There was nothing secret about anything I said" (Jn 18:19-20). Jesus had not neglected to instruct his disciples in private, but he had not kept his teaching or his claims to himself. He had often spoken so as to suggest that he was more than man (Jn 5:17f; 19-47; 8:14ff; 10:30-39). Now he insists on his rights. "Why do you ask me? The law does not require a man to testify against himself. Ask those who have heard me. It should be obvious that they will know what I have said." To have expounded his doctrine before his captors would have been fruitless.

It is an irony of history that the witnesses who testified against Jesus at his trial made charges against him that were obviously ridiculous. The gospel does not state precisely how or where the evidence was contradictory, but it may have centered about what Jesus had said when he drove the buyers and sellers from the Temple (Jn 2:19). He had not vowed to destroy the Temple, but had said that if his *body* were destroyed, he would raise it up in three days. He was misunderstood. Still, to tear down the Temple in order to rebuild it was not a crime; Herod the Great had done precisely that.

Jesus' calm words produced an impasse, and one of the guards, sensing the highpriest's embarrassment, struck the prisoner in the face. Jesus had said nothing impertient in denying his guilt, or in demanding that his trial be conducted legally. Early in his ministry, he had announced an end to the old law of an eye for an eye, but it was surely not his intention that victims of injustice be deprived of the right to speak out against injustice. "If I have spoken wrongly," he said steadily, "bear witness to the wrong, but if I have spoken rightly why do you strike me?" (Jn 18:23).

The highpriest was not disturbed by this blow. It was rather Jesus' words about destroying the Temple that he found disconcerting. Jesus seemed to imply that he had a power and authority greater than that holy building. Putting aside his role as impartial spectator and judge, the highpriest stood up and asked the prisoner: "Have you no answer to make? What is it that these men testify against you?" (Mk 15:60) Jesus remained silent. What could he say about conflicting evidence? He was under no obligation to make sense out of it. "Their testimony did not agree" (Mk 14-59).

The highpriest brought the interrogation to a climax: "Are you the Messiah, the Son of the Blessed One?" (15:61), he asked. These words actually contain two questions, for Messiah and Son of God were never, either in the Jewish mind of the time or in the Old Testament, interchangeable terms. Jesus might have claimed to be the Messiah, but many others had claimed that before and after his time without incurring official wrath. A Messiah might be guilty of delusions of grandeur, megalomania, or insanity, but not necessarily of blasphemy.

However, to claim to be the Son of God was another matter. Throughout the Old Testament the words "Son of God" were used in a wide variety of meanings, referring to the angels (Ps 28:1; Job 1:6); to men (Ex 4:22; Dt 1:31; Wis 18:13); to the Chosen People (Dt 14:1); to upright men (Sir 4:10; Wis 2:13); to princes and judges (Ps 81:7); to the king, God's anointed (2 Sm 7:14), and to the Messiah (Ps 2:7; 89). Caiaphas, a convinced monotheist, did not think that Jesus was either the Messiah or a true Son of God, but he sensed that Jesus considered himself as both. And so, in fact, did he answer the highpriest's question, "I am." Here was a reply straight as a pin, a categorical claim to be in truth the real Son of God. In Matthew, Jesus is said to reply, "It is you who say this" which indicates (as the papyrus evidence shows) an affirmative answer, but with reservations, perhaps something like, "Yes, but I shouldn't put it quite like that." He was saying that he was not the popular, all-conquering Messiah the people longed for, but a Son of God in a way that would safeguard the ancient revelation of monotheism. Jesus then alludes to two Old Testament texts to prove his point. They are: "The Lord said to my lord: 'Sit at my right hand' " (Ps 110:1), and "coming on the clouds of heaven, one like a son of man" (Dn 7:13). Jesus said, "You will see the Son of Man seated at the right hand of the Power and coming with the clouds of heaven" (Mt 26:64).

Jesus claimed a right to share God's glorious throne, and to possess and use divine power. That is, he claimed equality with the Father. This was a recognizable claim to divinity, and Jesus intended his words to be so understood.

The importance of Jesus' reply cannot be overemphasized. In claiming to be God and the Son of God as well as the Messiah, he had signed his own death warrant. Moslems, Unitarians, Jews, members of certain modern sects, and others who revere Jesus Christ, part company with Christians on this crucial point. Jesus knew that he was about to die, but he had no desire to die for the wrong reason. If he was to die, it would have to be for the right reason—because he claimed to be the Son of God.

On hearing Jesus' reply, the highpriest tore his garments in an age-old gesture of disapproval, disavowal, indignant protest, grief, and rejection of what had just been said (Gn 37:30; 1 Mc 2:14; 4:39; Lv 10:6; 21:10). No need now for further witnesses; all had heard the "blasphemy." The original charge of planning to destroy the Temple was dropped, and Caiaphas made the most of the prisoner's open and shocking claim. " 'You have heard the blasphemy. What is your verdict?' And they all condemned his as liable to death."

Mark and Matthew stress the fact that the true cause for Jesus' condemnation was the attitude of the Jewish leaders to his claim to divinity. Their grievance was thus of a religious order. However, the verdict of the Sanhedrin constituted only a judicial opinion: the death penalty was reserved to the Roman procurator, and he was not likely to impose it to settle a Jewish religious dispute. The next step in the proceedings was to induce the procurator to ratify the Sanhedrin's decision without, if possible, alluding to the true nature of the grievance. The charge which was eventually formulated and presented to Pilate cleverly masked the religious motive behind the condemnation of Jesus.

While Jesus' enemies were inside Caiaphas' house conspiring to manipulate the procurator, another drama was unfolding in the courtyard outside.

Peter's Denials

The highly dramatic story of Peter's denial of his Master has etched itself indelibly on the mind of western man. These denials are included in the gospel record to remind us of the ever-present dangers of apostasy, and the narrative surely reflects the reminiscences of Peter himself. Details are related with perfect candor, and the psychological appropriateness of Peter's various responses to remarks addressed to him corresponds to what we know of him.

John explains how Peter was able to gain entry into the courtyard of the highpriest. "Simon Peter kept following [the verbal form denotes action still in progress] in company with another disciple" (Jn 18:15). The other disciple is usually identified as John, who hides his identity throughout the fourth gospel. The early Fathers of the Church thought that John was acquainted with the highpriest and was a man of some culture and education. He was able to gain entrance to the court without attracting undue attention to himself. Not so Peter. One can almost picture John moving about inside contacting the proper persons about his friend, and assuring the servant girl that it would be all right if she permitted his friend Peter to come in.

In the inner court, a group of people were gathered around a small fire. Nights in the Palestinian spring are chilly, especially after a rain. Jerusalem is not only 2,600 feet above sea level, but it is also close to the desert, which is cold at night. Peter edged into the group around the glowing embers, outwardly just another man. The very ordinariness of his action gave no indication of the turbulence of his thoughts. He succeeded in going unnoticed for a few moments. Perhaps it was when someone threw a bundle of reeds or thorns upon the coals that the fire flared up (Lk 22:56). The servant girl caught a good look at his face, looked again, and then cried out excitedly, "You also were with Jesus the Galilean!" (Mt 26:69). The sentence in Greek (*kai su meta tou Nazarenou estha tou Jesou!*) suggests an excited, unrehearsed outburst.

Peter's answer was equally unrehearsed and prompt. He said the first thing that came to his mind, and his reply is the confused answer of a man caught completely by surprise. "I don't know really," or, "I don't understand what you are saying" (*ouk oida ti legeis*, Mk 14:68). Peter would undoubtedly have given a much better account of himself if he had been physically attacked, but trading words was not his forte. To the end of his days he would be sensitive to what others were thinking (Gal 2:11) and now he flinched at the question and sought to escape, pretending that he had not understood. It was evasive action. In substance, however, he denied the charge (Jn 18:17), and as he did so he began to edge out of the courtyard, making his way toward the vestibule, fearful naturally for his safety, but unwilling to tear himself entirely from the scene.

Thanks to Mark's observation that Peter was below in the courtyard (66), it is possible to conclude that Jesus was being interrogated in an upper room.

One would not expect the courtyard of the highpriest's house to be brilliantly lighted. As Peter, hoping to avoid further embarrassment, was edging toward the door, seeking out the darker areas, a cock crowed (Mk 14:66). If Peter heard it, he may have told himself rather uncomfortably that he had not after all explicitly denied his Master, but had only dodged the question. His comfort was to be of brief duration as, out of the half-darkness, he heard the charge, "You also are one of them" (Lk 22:58). John framed this accusation as a question, "Are not you also one of this man's disciples?" (Jn 18:17). In either case it is clear that Jesus was so much in everyone's mind that the words "this man" sufficed to identify him. Mark notes that Peter denied it "again"; the first evasion then must also be construed as a denial.

After a short interval (Luke puts it about an hour later), Peter was faced with a third accusation. Something he had muttered or said must have sounded odd to the people in the courtyard, and he was prodded into further speech. Suspicion quickly became a certainty: this man was a Galilean. The bystanders thereupon took up the maidservant's words and said, "you are certainly one of them! You are a Galilean, are you not?" The country bumpkins from the north had, it seems, a peculiarity of accent that was easily recognizable. To illustrate: If a Galilean were to speak, he might be asked derisively whether he was saying *hamor* (ass), or *amar* (wool), or *hamar* (wine), or *immar* (lamb). Modern Galileans, too, have these speech peculiarities. Near Nazareth one day, an Arab asked P. Benoit, the leader of our little expedition from the Ecole Biblique, "Where are you from?" and the answer was, of course,

"From Jerusalem." In Arabic, Jerusalem is called el-Quds, or "The Holy City." The Arab looked puzzled for a moment, and then his face cleared. "Ah," he said, "min el-'uds!," pronouncing the "q" so deeply in his throat as to lose it entirely. The Galilean accent still holds, twenty centuries later!

Jesus had once said, "Simon, Simon, take heed. Satan has been given leave to sift you all like wheat. But I have prayed for you, that your faith may not fail. . . . You in turn must strengthen your brothers" (Lk 22:31f). Satan was now sifting and the experience was not pleasant. With oaths and curses Peter shouted loudly, "I do not know the man you are talking about" (Mk 14:71). One last scruple prevented him from pronouncing the name of Jesus.

At this point the tension must have been extremely high, and the silence electric. Into that silence sharp and piercing as a knife there came the sound of a cock crowing the second time. It was probably close to 5 a.m. (Jn 18:28). Jesus came forth from the judgment hall, turned and looked at Peter (Lk 22:61), who then broke down and wept tears of sorrow (Mt 26:75). Not for him the barren regret of a Judas. Disappointing as his denials were, Peter's faith in and love for Jesus had never wavered. That, at least, may be what his tears betoken. Matthew speaks of three denials, noting in them the mounting intensity: first a simple denial, then oaths, cursing, and swearing. It is practically impossible to harmonize the accounts of Peter's denials. If the variations are all maintained, Peter denied his Master seven times. But the tradition as to the number three, predicted by Jesus himself, is firm. The difference in details do not touch the substance of the account, and may simply reflect the differences in each author's style.

There are other unanswered questions arising from the story of Peter's denials. It is strange that Peter alone, and not John, was so put on the spot. Mark 14:67, "You also" is intriguing. Was John also questioned? Also, what was Peter's sin, precisely? One might charge him with a formidable array of sins: presumption, fear, cowardice, dishonesty, perjury, blasphemy, and imprudence. The circumstances of his denials, however, must have diminished somewhat the seriousness of his failure.

In later years, as we can deduce from the gospel accounts (especially Mark's), Peter exhibited a remarkable candor and humility. Even on that fateful night Peter was capable of true repentance. "Going out, he wept bitterly" (Mt 26:75).

The Indignities

Peter denied his Master during the night-questioning of Jesus in the house of the highpriest. After they finished questioning Jesus, his enemies debated how to present the case to the Roman procurator. While they conspired, they had the prisoner led away.

Several hours may yet have remained until dawn. They were long hours for the prisoner, for his guards began to mock him and beat him. The soldiers spat upon him, struck him in the face with the back of their hands, perhaps also with their fists (Mt 26:67). The blindfolded prisoner was taunted for pretending to be a prophet. It has been held by some that this covering of the prisoner's face was Roman practice, but since the perpetrators were the temple police and the incident occurred in the highpriest's house, such an explanation is unlikely. Balaam began to prophesy with his eyes closed (Nm 24:4) or perhaps Jesus' head was covered after the fashion of the later Arab diviners, who hid their faces when about to deliver their oracles. The clear intention of the guards was anything but respectful. The victim was struck, then derisively asked to identify his striker. Some situations promote coarse behavior.

Actually, there seem to have been five scenes of outrage, but they can be reduced to three: the first at the hands of the night guards and the Sanhedrin (Luke and Mark/Matthew), a second at Herod's court (Lk 23:11), and the last at Pilate's court.

Morning Session Before the Sanhedrin

It has struck many as strange that although Luke describes Jesus' appearance before the Sanhedrin in the early morning hours (22:66), Matthew and Mark describe two meetings of that august body—one at night and one in the morning. Neither Luke nor John mention the death sentence passed on Christ, but they both presuppose it. It seems clear that there were two meetings of the Sanhedrin, for John puts one before Annas and the other before Caiaphas. Apparently, Luke has simplified and clarified the course of events. The Sanhedrin would naturally have wanted to make sure it had the right man as prisoner, and thus had asked him a few questions during the night. For Luke a night meeting could hardly have been the official one; the session that really counted was the one in the morning. Matthew, like Mark, has only a single verse for the morning session, but states nevertheless that it was held for the purpose of condemning Christ to death; here he may be echoing Luke.

In all probability, the death sentence was not pronounced on Jesus until morning. The Sanhedrin was made up of high-priests and scribes and they met in their hall of deliberation. Luke does not refer to the Temple or to the false witnesses. The questioning now centered on the title "Christ" or "Messiah," for this was an angle that had to be made clear. "Tell us, are you the Messiah?" (Lk 22:66). Jesus answered with a marvelous calm; he understood that they had no intention of listening, or of believing what he said. "If I tell you, you will not believe me," he replied. "And if I question you, you will not answer." These people would not listen. What chance did he now have with them as his judges? His words are similar to Jeremiah's before the hostile king Zedekiah (38:15), except that Jesus' complaint is the loftier. One senses that Jesus does not refuse the claim to be the Messiah, but he understands the term differently from his interrogators. They shall have their answer, however, and they shall know what kind of Messiah he is. "This much only will I say: 'From now on, the Son of Man will have his seat at the right hand of the Power of God' " (Lk 22:69). Luke is shorter here than Matthew and Mark; he omits the part about the coming on clouds, but keeps the figure (seated at the right hand. . .), which expresses his glory. Jesus' answer stressed the abiding reality of his relationship with God.

The members of the Sanhedrin all (Lk) jumped on his reply, and pushed him further: "So you are the Son of God then?" Jesus referred to himself as the Son of Man, but the inference that he was making himself the Son of God, was difficult to miss. Jesus maintained that he was indeed the Son of God, but not in a simplistic fashion. His reply, "It is you who say I am," was not an attack on the belief in one God, but his listeners took his claim to be blasphemy, deserving of death. Once this point had been made, there was nothing more to say. "Need we call further witnesses? We have heard it from his own lips." Luke did not feel it necesary to spell out the explicit condenmation.

The Roman Trial

The Procurator, Pontius Pilate

The story of Pontius Pilate, the fifth of twelve procurators to govern the province of Judaea, is part of the story of man's salvation. He is mentioned in the gospels and in the Creed. Pilate, like Judas, represents everyman who, knowing what is right and what is just, toys with danger, is maneuvered from compromise to compromise, until his only "salvation" lies in an act of gross injustice. That others might suffer from his action meant little to him. Pilate's story is, in miniature, the disturbing story of every man who comes into Jesus' presence.

Among ancient writers, only Tertullian treated Pilate with consideration, imagining him to be a Christian at heart. Did he not thrice declare publicly of Christ: "I find no cause in him"? In the Abysinnian Church, the feast of (St.) Pilate is celebrated on June 25th; the Greek Church honors his wife, Procula, on October 27th. Anatole France, however, portrays Pilate differently in one of his stories. He has Pilate reminiscing to a friend about a famous Nazarean wonderworker whom he had had crucified. At the end of the interesting story, Pilate's friend asked who this man was, and what was his name. Typically, Pilate replied, "I don't remember." He probably would not have.

Pilate was not of the Roman nobility, but of the equestrian order. In the discharge of his duties as procurator he was immediately answerable to the legate of Syria; Syria was an imperial province. Besides seeing to maintaining order in the turbulent province of Judea, the procurator's chief task was to insure the collection of taxes for the imperial treasury. This tax was called the *fiscus,* to distinguish it from the senatorial *aerarium.*

Our sources tell us that Pilate was an obstinate, unyielding man whose administration was marked by imprudence and displays of bad judgment. In his ten years as governor of Judea (26-36 A.D.), he acquired a reputation for corruption, violence, robbery, and harshness in his treatment of people. He was a man given to wanton and constant cruelty.

Pilate's first official act did not endear him to the Jews. On the occasion of a religious festival, he brought troops into Jerusalem by night with military standards flying. He thus showed his indifference to the religious sensibilities of the Jews, who interpreted the action as a deliberate violation of the first commandment—"You shall not make for yourself a graven image" (Ex 20:4). The Jews took this as a deliberate insult, and for the next five days, kept the city in a positive turmoil with public manifestations of disapproval and indignation at the procurator's action. Delegation after delegation was sent to the imperial headquarters, and in the end, if only to restore order to the city, Pilate ordered the removal of the offending images.

On another occasion Pilate introduced into Jerusalem a number of golden shields inscribed with the Emperor's name, and displayed them on the walls of his headquarters. If this incident is not a variant of the one mentioned above, Pilate showed that he knew little about public relations. Jewish protests on this occasion were heard in far off Rome, and it is said that Tiberius personally rebuked the procurator and ordered him to remove the offending shields and transfer them to the pagan temple in Caesarea. This incident may have occurred about 31 A.D.

There was another blunder of an even more serious nature. Without consultation with the local authorities, apparently, and perhaps thinking that he was doing something to benefit both city and people, Pilate began the construction of an aqueduct to bring water from near Bethlehem to the city and to the Temple. The project was in fact a good one, for Jerusalem suffered from a chronic shortage of water (Gihon is the only fresh-water spring in the city: cisterns supply most of its water, or did, until the Israelis piped it in from the Sea of Galilee). But Pilate blundered by laying his hands on Temple funds to pay for the aqueduct, funds contributed by the faithful for the up-keep of the Temple and the holy place. Popular resentment at the procurator's highhanded methods was not slow in coming but Pilate was ready for it. Soldiers disguised as pilgrims infiltrated the crowds, and at a given signal beat the demonstrators with clubs that had been concealed beneath cloaks. The critics were thus brutally silenced, but the incident could hardly have been forgotten. John's account of Jesus' trial allows the reader to feel the mutual dislike and distrust between the procurator and the people.

On still another occasion (ca. 35 A.D.), Pilate learned that a large crowd had assembled on Mount Garizim in Samaria, drawn by the promise of a "prophet" that he would show them the sacred vessels of Moses' time. Pilate again resorted to harsh measures, and his soldiers dispersed the crowd with brutal ferocity. This was another blunder. The outraged Samaritans appealed to Vitellius, the Syrian legate, and he sent Pilate to Rome to stand trial for his conduct. However, the emperor Tiberius died before the trial could take place and Pilate simply disappears from history.

The Roman trial of Jesus, especially as related in the Fourth Gospel, conveys to the reader something of the tension existing between judicial Rome and judicial Judaism. The story is an excellent example of John's skill as a narrator. There is a great deal of movement (Pilate goes in and out of the pretorium many times), and the dialogue is charged with layers of passion and meaning.

At the Praetorium

Early in the morning (perhaps around 6:00 a.m.) Jesus was led, securely bound (Mk 15:1), to the hall of the procurator. He was accompanied by the police escort appointed by the Sanhedrin, and by members of the Sanhedrin, whose night's work had to be brought to a successful conclusion.

The tent in which the procurator took up his headquarters was called the Praetorium. It was the official residence of the Roman praetor. Its exact location remains somewhat unclear. Certainly the tent gave way to a building, and many identify this with the Antonia. Originally built by Herod the Great (B.C. 37-4) and named in honor of Marc Antony, this military garrison occupied the northwest corner of the Temple area, a place where feelings ran high and trouble could and did easily develop. This Antonia was well-situated; from it, Roman soldiers could quickly descend the two sets of stairs leading into the Temple area and quell trouble before it got out of hand. (Paul was saved by such an intervention [Acts 21:31]).

Another possible site for the Praetorium is the palace of Herod the Great, or the Citadel (El Qalaa), an imposing ruin just to the south of the present Jaffa Gate. From 6 A.D. on, this castle had normally served as the residence of Roman procurators when they came to Jerusalem from Caesarea. The present structure owes much to Suleiman the Magnificent, who embellished it at the time the present south wall of the city was constructed (1532). Here, in 24 B.C., Herod had built three towers, named Hippicus, Phasael, and Mariamne. They were left standing when Titus destroyed the city in 70 A.D., but were totally demolished when Hadrian crushed the Second Jewish Revolt (132-135 A.D.) sixty years later. Under Hadrian, a great builder, the city was completely remodeled along Roman lines and given the name of Aelia Capitolina, by which it was known for almost 200 years.

Where then was the Praetorium? The Antonia and the Citadel are equidistant from Golgotha, and the probabilities in favor of either site are about equal. John (19:13) noted that Jesus was pronounced guilty in a place called Lithostrotos (in Hebrew, Gabbatha). The discovery of huge stone blocks, well-scored and rutted by wheels, in the basement of the present convent of the Dames de Sion, suggests that the Praetorium was close by the Antonia, since the convent is near the Temple area. But this pavement may have been the work of Hadrian's engineers and hence no older than 135 A.D. On the other hand, the term *lithostrotos* also describes a sort of mosaic, and from

the mosaics found in the Citadel during the course of archaeological investigations there, one might conclude that the Pretorium was located on the west side of the city.

So the debate rages on. Years ago, Fathers Vincent and
Abel, great friends and the archaeological and geographical
experts at the Ecole Biblique, found it impossible to agree on
the location of the Praetorium. As a result, when they made
the Stations of the Cross, P. Vincent began his at the Antonia,
while P. Abel began his from the Citadel—from opposite ends
of the city.

The Praetorium bears on the question of the day of Jesus'
death. As John remarks (18:23) the Jews would not enter this
pagan building with their prisoners before the Passover. Since
it was a building from which the leaven had not been removed,
contact with it would render them legally impure and disbar
them from eating the passover meal that evening. How strange
that men can be preoccupied with minor infractions of law,
and suffer no qualms about greater sins.

Pilate, responsible for law and order in the city, was up early
that momentous day (Jn 18:28). He was surely well-informed
about what was going on. The Jews had come with a prisoner,
so Pilate went forth from the Praetorium to see the man's accusers. His opening words were blunt and to the point, "What
accusation do you bring against this man?" The recognized
procedure had to be followed: everything had to be spelled out
for the record. No charge, no trial.

The First Charge: Jesus is a Criminal

Taken aback by Pilate's brusque demand for a charge whose
validity would be weighed by civil authority, Jesus' accusers
tried to evade the issue. "If this man were not an evildoer we
would not have handed him over." Here was a blatant attempt
to gain a conviction without having to disclose the reasons for
their request. Pilate recognized the ruse, and also sensed that
he was being used. He was not disposed to play the game that
way. With heavy irony, he elaborately pretended to believe
that the case involved some question of the Law over which
their own courts had jurisdiction. "Take him yourselves and

judge him by your own law" (v. 31a). Pilate meant that he would not judge the case unless he knew what it was all about.

Pilate's harsh reply was a reminder to the Jews of the galling restrictions which Rome had imposed on their jurisdictional rights. Their grudging admission "It is not lawful for us to put any man to death" meant that the *jus gladii* had been taken from them. To obtain the death penalty, they had decided to present the case in such a way as to suggest that, in the course of a trial, they had learned of an offense deserving of capital punishment. The transition from a religious to a political charge was simply brilliant. Jesus is now represented to the procurator as a disturber of the public peace, and as a fomenter of rebellion. "We found this man perverting our nation and forbidding us to give tribute to Caesar, and calling himself the Messiah, a king" (Lk 23:2).

All these things, John reports, took place that the word of Jesus might be fulfilled, signifying the kind of death he was to die (Jn 18:32).

The Second Charge: Jesus is a King

To the annoyance of his petitioners, Pilate had clarified the question of competence, that is, he had forced a grudging though indirect admission that he alone had authority in capital criminal cases. He entered the hall to interview the prisoner. Perhaps he thought that he had to deal with another bothersome pretender to the throne of Israel; there was seemingly an unending supply of such dreamers. He plied the prisoner with questions, probably in Greek, the common language of the ancient world. He was of course concerned to learn if there were ground for official worry about a national outbreak of anti-Roman feeling, and bluntly asked the prisoner, "Are you the King of the Jews?" (Jn 18:33).

Jesus had been kept within the Praetorium while Pilate was outside (v.29) talking, and had not therefore heard the accusations made against him. Pilate's question, "Are you the king of the Jews?" was a dangerous one, almost meaning "Are you a rebel?" An unqualified affirmative would have been self-condemnatory, so Jesus answered with the question, "Do you say this of your own accord or did others say it to you about me?" His answer would depend upon the source of the question.

Pilate became annoyed at this unexpected answer, although the Roman in him must have appreciated the prisoner's desire to know exactly where he stood before answering. He answered, "Am I a Jew? Your own nation and their chief priests have handed you over to me. What have you done?" The statements sound harsh and blunt, as if the procurator resented the implication that he had no mind of his own. Pilate may also have been irritated because he was beginning to suspect that everything was not as it appeared on the surface. Ordinarily the Jews were only too willing to rally about anyone who would strike a blow for their liberty, yet here they were demanding the death of this "king." "What have you done?" he demanded irritably.

"My kingdom does not belong to this world," Jesus answered. "If it did, my subjects would be fighting to save me from arrest by the Jews. But my kingdom is not of this kind" (Jn 18:36). These words, in which Jesus described his kingdom in negative fashion, told Pilate the real reason why Jesus' own people hated him. Jesus wanted no part of a popular uprising, but rather insisted on his spiritual sovereignty in a spiritual kingdom. No wonder the Jewish priests hated him. They had cause for worry, but Pilate had no worries. He must have smiled, seeing that he was not dealing with a revolutionary agitator or pretender to the throne of Israel. That Jesus considered himself a spiritual king was in Pilate's eyes insignificant enough; it stamped the prisoner as a harmless dreamer. However, to safeguard the Emperor's sovereignty, he asked the prisoner, with some irony, "So, then, you are a king?" omitting the phrase "of the Jews" with which he had begun his interrogation (v. 33).

"King is your word," Jesus replied. It was not a simple acceptance of what Pilate had said nor a denial of fact, but rather a qualified "Yes." Jesus had never claimed to be merely a king. King was not an accurate description of his role or of his person, but just the same, he was a king. He could not truthfully deny that he was.

In saying, "if my kingdom were of this world," Jesus was stating that his kingdom was not of this world. Now he explained further that his kingdom was one of truth, and that his followers are men who love the truth. "For this was I born; for this I came into the world, to bear witness to the truth. Anyone committed to the truth hears my voice." Truth is his realm. He has not only established its borders, he is in fact its boundary. Anyone who hears his voice, that is, anyone who accepts and appreciates and obeys what he says, belongs to him. Never has another religious teacher made such a claim to the acceptance and allegiance of all who are concerned with truth. Jesus is king of the people of God. He is the Savior. Having said this, Jesus fell silent. Pilate's "Truth? What is that?" drew no answer from him.

Pilate was annoyed. This could hardly have been the first time he had had to deal with a wise man who claimed to have a special grasp on truth. For such men, he had no sympathy, nor was he interested in them. Jesus appeared to be a philosopher or madman; at any rate, he was not dangerous. Pilate's question was not a sincere quest for truth, but it was not exactly flippant either. It was perhaps a kind of idle repetition of a word or phrase used by another, an echo of Jesus' words about truth. Pilate's question had been answered: Jesus was not politically ambitious. One can almost see him muttering "Truth? What is that?" over his shoulder as he turned away. Obviously, this was not the time for philosophical discussion.

Going out of the Praetorium and addressing the men who had accused Jesus, Pilate announced the result of his interrogation. "Speaking for myself," he said, "I find no case against this man." But the priests and elders resisted this verdict. Ultimately, Pilate's weakness, not his convictions, led him to hand Jesus to his death.

Jesus Before Herod Antipas

Pilate suddenly had a brilliant idea. Hearing Jesus described as a Galilean, the procurator decided to send the Nazarene to the tetrarch of Galilee, who was then in Jerusalem, and let *him* deal with the case. The tetrarch was Herod Antipas, a petty king whom Jesus had once scathingly referred to as "that fox" (Lk 13:32) and who had distinguished himself by keeping a drunken promise to have John the Baptist beheaded.

Pilate must have considered this move a master stroke, for there had been a coolness between himself and the tetrarch ever since Pilate caused the death of some Galilean pilgrims (Lk 13:1). Details concerning this incident are wanting, but the incident probably involved the Roman garrison watching over the Temple area during some religious festival. Pilate was not as a rule an indirect man, but from a political point of view his sending Jesus to Herod was very shrewd. The gesture might soothe Herod's ruffled feelings, and that petty king might hit upon some way of solving Pilate's problem.

Herod was in fact more than pleased at Pilate's gesture, since it afforded him the opportunity to satisfy his curiosity about Jesus. Was he really John the Baptist risen from the dead, or Elijah or some other wonderworker (Lk 9:7–9)? He met Jesus with a torrent of questions about his mission. But Jesus remained silent, for Herod was not disposed to profit from what he had to say. Jesus never consented to be the object of mere curiosity; he welcomed only earnest seekers and lovers of truth.

Herod would not tolerate Jesus' silence. John the Baptist had appeared before him; it had cost him his head (Mt 14:3–12). Herod could not execute Jesus while the Roman procurator was in command of the city, but he would take other revenge—he would treat Jesus as a lunatic enthusiast. He ordered a gala robe to be wrapped about the prisoner, as if giving assent to his claim to be king. The meaning of the gesture was clear to all: here is a fool. Herod's court and guard of honor echoed his laughter at the comic king. The temple guards had mocked Jesus the night before; this time the mockery was official. Men fear laughter more than they do blows, but Jesus maintained an impressive silence. In the face of his silence, the sport fell flat, so Herod sent him back to Pilate.

Finding the prisoner once more on his hands, Pilate must have appreciated, sourly, the clever way Herod had handled the situation. But something had been gained—the prisoner had been only mocked, not condemned. Pilate would make two further attempts to free Jesus, trying to gain his release through a custom proper to the festival time. Meanwhile, as a concession to the crowd, he would have him scourged.

As he summoned the hierarchy and people to him, Pilate may have had it in mind to play one off against the other. His words were direct and to the point. "You have brought this man before me as one who subverts the people. I have examined him in your presence and have found nothing in him to support your charges. Neither did Herod, for he sent him back to us. Clearly this man has done nothing that deserves death. Therefore I mean to release him, once I have taught him a lesson" (Lk 23:14–16).

Pilate's decision to have Jesus scourged was highly irregular. Scourging was the normal preliminary to crucifixion, and followed the pronouncing of sentence. The word used by Pilate (*paideuein*, to discipline) was a terrible euphemism, chosen perhaps as a sop to his conscience, masking the flagrant injustice of the procedure. Actually, this scourging was a capitulation to Jesus' accusers. The procurator was not squeamish about physical punishment. If the prisoner were innocent, scourging would not hurt him over much, but if he was involved in anything questionable, the punishment would be painful enough to make him think twice about disturbing the peace again.

Pilate looked tough, but he was caving in to the pressures on him. He had violated regular procedure by having Jesus scourged, and the Jews instantly recognized Pilate's concession for the sordid compromise it was. They assumed, correctly as it would turn out, that he could be pushed even further.

The Choice of Barabbas

All four evangelists mention a peculiar custom connected with the festival time (John limits it to the Passover, 18:39). As a gesture of clemency, a prisoner was released. This token of Roman generosity is known to us only from the gospels, although Livy (V:13) speaks about an entertainment of the gods (*lectisternium*), a pardon (*indulgentia*), and an annulment (*abolitio*), which are all similar.

Barabbas is known only from the gospel accounts. A notorious robber (*lestes*), he was languishing in jail at the time on charges of riot and murder (Mk 15:7). Imagine the irony of a choice between Jesus or Barabbas? The crowd that Pilate faced was doubtless inclined in Barabbas' favor (Mt 27:15). Zealous Jews would admire any gesture of revolt or defiance of Roman authority. The release of a prisoner was a traditional privilege, and the crowd came up to the Praetorium (Mk 15:8) to see that it was honored. Nothing is said as to the size of the crowd, or whether it was originally for or against Jesus, or whether, composed of Zealots (the national firebrands), it was for Barabbas. But the crowd knew what it wanted: the release of a prisoner during Passover.

There next occurred a miracle of clumsiness on Pilate's part. Instead of simply releasing Jesus, Pilate could not resist asking a malicious question: "Do you want me to release for you the King of the Jews?" The contempt was obvious; this "king," standing before them in bonds, was an open object of riducule. Pilate was thus deliberately mocking the Jewish priests. He knew that the prisoner had been handed over to him because the priests were upset by his reputation and popularity, and he thought that the people would support one who had so recently entered the city in triumph. But Pilate misjudged the situation badly. Moreover, his question indicated that justice meant little to him. No judge should expose an innocent man to the mercies of the mob, especially when it might make the wrong choice. This mob would do just that.

As Pilate approached his judgment bench, a message from his wife reached him. He and she had possibly been discussing the prisoner, and their conversation carried over into a dream she had concerning "that holy" man (Jesus). She implored her husband to do nothing against him. Her plea recalls that of Calpurnia to her husband Julius Caesar about the Ides of March. Pilate might well have felt uneasy about the coincidence, but, like Caesar, he chose to go stubbornly ahead. The message and his reaction to it must have taken some time, and the priests used the interval to stir up the crowd. Pilate's wife is called Procula in the apocryphal letter of Pilate to Herod, and a tradition in the Greek Church holds that she became a Christian.

The sight of Jesus stung the Jews to a resentment that was quickly fanned into flame by the chief priests. Pilate had badly miscalculated the extent and depth of Jewish national pride. Confident that the crowd would choose Jesus of Nazareth, he was stunned when the crowd burst into a wild clamor for Barabbas. "Then what shall I do with Jesus, who is called Christ?" (Mt 27:22). Under the circumstances it was not a good question, for the reply to it was, "Away with this man, and release to us Barabbas!" Repeated chanting of "Crucify him, crucify him," precluded further discussion. In attempting to cope with this insistent cry for blood, Pilate again revealed his weakness.

"Why? What evil had he done? I have found in him no crime deserving death." Bewildered now, Pilate began to doubt his own previous judgment. This man may be guilty of something, but not of anything calling for death. Pilate's protests are interesting: "I do not find a case. . . " (Lk 23:4), "Neither has Herod . . . [he] has done nothing that calls for death" (v. 15); "I have not discovered anything that calls for death" (v. 22). In the end, however, Pilate released Barabbas to appease the crowd.

One can picture Barabbas, excited and exhilarated at his sudden release and popularity, and then the slow realization that in fact there was another who was the center of all attention and interest—Jesus of Nazareth. Nothing is known of the fate of Barabbas.

The Scourging

Josephus twice notes that scourging was the normal preliminary to crucifixion. The victim was bound to a pillar in a slightly stooped position, immobilized so that his body would receive the full force of the flagellum upon his back. This whip was of leather thongs, each of which was studded with sharp bits of bone or metal (hence aptly named *scorpions*). Scourging was administered by two, or at times four or six men, and not infrequently resulted in the victim's death. Horace and Cicero supply us with grisly details about this horrible punishment. Luke alone among the evangelists does not mention it.

Two pillars of the scourging have been venerated by believers. One of them is in the Franciscan chapel adjoining the Church of the Resurrection in Jerusalem. The other is in S. Praxedis, in Rome.

The Crowning With Thorns

Jesus was led into the Praetorium where, Mark tells us (15:16), the whole cohort was assembled. By this he doubtless meant that all who were available at the moment—a platoon, perhaps, or a company—were assembled there. Throughout the Roman Empire, Jews were exempt from military duty, for their stubborn insistence on Sabbath observance, even when on campaign, made their support uncertain in military operations. The soldiers Mark speaks of were probably Romans and Samaritans. Contemptuous of the Jews to begin with, they were devoid of pity for the bloody prisoner now put into their custody. On seeing that Herod had derisively clad him in a royal robe, they carried on the jest, improvising mock honors for Jesus.

The soldiers stripped the prisoner of his royal robe, and threw a soldier's scarlet cloak about his shoulders. The color was a shoddy imitation of the royal purple. A reed thrust into his hands suggested a scepter, but the soldiers would snatch it away and strike him with it. The Temple soldiery had spat upon and struck Jesus; the Romans reversed the process, first bending the knee before him, then spitting upon him. The whole proceeding was one of deliberate mockery and insult.

"They wove a crown of thorns and put it on him" (Mk 15:17). The crown was probably a grotesque bonnet of crisscrossed stems of pimpernel, a thorny shrub which grows around Jerusalem. It was extensively used for firewood, and the soldiers had quantities of it on hand for the fire which was kept burning during the night. The crowning with thorns was not a special torture, but a not-so-subtle form of derision.

After a time, the scarlet cloak was removed and Jesus was clothed in his own garments.

Pilate's Last Attempt to Release Jesus

One of the most dramatic moments in the gospel occurs in John 19:4–15. Trying to show that the prisoner had been sufficiently punished for whatever it was he was supposed to have done (Pilate was never clear about what this was), the procurator had Jesus brought into full view of the crowd, possibly on an upper story balcony, wearing the crown of thorns and Herod's cloak of royal purple. The emphatic repetition of these details is striking. Pointing to the prisoner, Pilate proclaimed to the crowd: "here is the man!"

These words were not well chosen, and were not likely to arouse the crowd's better sentiments. What Pilate meant to say was, you see before you a mere man who, for all his pretended royalty, is quite harmless. He implied that the representative of Rome was not frightened by so sorry a figure.

However, like Caiaphas on another occasion, Pilate had unwittingly hit upon a profound truth. Here is a series of striking contrasts. Dressed as a king, Jesus is presented as a prisoner. He claimed to be Son of God, but is declared to be a man. He is the object of pity or contempt, and of love and worship. This man is also the Son of God.

The matter appeared in quite another light to the leaders of the people, the priests who were mingled in the crowd. Sensing that Pilate was mocking them, they began loudly to cry, "Crucify him!" The case, ostensibly put into Roman hands, was to be decided by themselves. But Pilate could be stubborn too, and retorted with some heat, "Take him yourselves and crucify him, for I find no crime in him." He knew that they would not dare to inflict even their own form of capital punishment (stoning) upon the prisoner. Had they done so, he had only to lift a finger, and they would swiftly be taught a lesson of obedience and respect for Rome.

The Jewish leaders thus understood that Pilate had not really granted them anything. However greatly they wanted Jesus' death, it was in Pilate's power to thwart them. They therefore attempted to persuade him to look on things from their point of view. Their Law took a serious view of blasphemy (Lv 24:16), and Pilate should respect that Law and see to it that others did so as well. But then for the first time in Pilate's presence, the true grievance was allowed to emerge: "He made himself the Son of God."

On hearing these words, Pilate was more afraid than ever. To mistreat one sent by the gods was a dangerous business. Had not Bacchus recently appeared at Thebes, in Egypt? Had not Procula had a dream (Mt 27:19)? Returning to the prisoner, Pilate asked him, "Where are you from?" The question does not mean, exactly, are you of divine origin (Pilate would not so openly have displayed his credulity), but it left room for an answer that suggested divine origin.

Like the people at Cana (2:9), the Samaritan woman (4:11), the Apostles and the crowds (6:5), the Jewish leaders (7:27; 8:14; 9:29), Pilate was face to face with the mystery of Jesus, the focus of the whole gospel (16:28; 17:25). Jesus is, and has always been both the known, and the unknown. He made no reply to Pilate, who had shown himself to be uninterested in Truth. Augustine wrote, "When Christ is silent, he is silent as a lamb; when he speaks, he teaches as a shepherd." Pilate grew annoyed at Jesus' silence, and angrily shouted, "You will not speak to me? Do you not know that I have the power to release you, and power to crucify you" (Jn 19:10)? In other words, "Be silent before Herod and before those people out there if you wish, but not when I talk to you. I have real power."

Pilate was claiming to be able to do as he wished in matters of justice, and in so doing he was clearly wrong. As procurator, his duty was to administer justice fairly, not to indulge in personal whim. With a marvelous calm, Jesus corrected him. "You would have no power (*oudemian*, "none at all") over me unless it had been given you from above." Because he happened to be the Emperor's delegate, the procurator could deal with secular affairs, but he could not lawfully exercise power over Jesus unless God had willed it, and permitted it. Pilate's power was not his own, and his fault lies in the fact that he acted against his own conscience, and condemned an innocent man.

Jesus went on: "He who delivered me to you has the greater sin." Of whom was he speaking? Judas had not delivered him to Pilate. But Judas is surely not excluded here. P. Lagrange considers 19:11b as an "aside," emphasizing the fact that Judas was the traitor par excellence, and the most guilty of all those involved.

Jesus' words so impressed the procurator that he felt a kind of superstitious anxiety; he rushed outside, once again resolved to free the prisoner. Unfortunately, that was no longer possible. The moment he tried to do so, the priests dropped all formal civil and religious charges against the prisoner and struck without warning at Pilate's weakest spot. "If you release this man, you are not Caesar's friend."

Pilate was trapped. He realized at once that such a charge, if lodged against him before the Emperor, spelled an end to his career, perhaps his life as well. He knew from past experience that the Jews would not hesitate to go right to the top. To be a "friend of Caesar" (*Amicus Caesaris*) meant unquestioned loyalty to the Emperor at all times. The prime duty of governors of provinces was to be zealous in maintaining the rights of the Emperor. The Jews would whisper into Tiberius' suspicious ear about Pilate's indulgence toward a claimant to royalty, and Pilate would be guilty of lèse majesté. Pilate could not take the chance. Rome was not liable to be displeased with a man who showed zeal for the Empire. If in that zeal an innocent man or two should lose his life, *that* might be regretted, but it would be understood.

Pilate brought Jesus outside again, and himself sat down on the judgment bench (*bema*) at a place called Lithostrotos (Gabbatha in Hebrew). The text here allows for some interesting speculation as to whether Pilate or the prisoner sat upon the bema. It might be argued that Jesus was made to sit upon the bench, to lend dramatic force to Pilate's words, "Here is your king" (19:14). It would provide a parallel to verses 2, 3, and 5, and would explain why Pilate did not pronounce the sentence on Christ. On the other hand, the verb (*kathizein*) is intransitive (he does not make the prisoner sit down on it), nor indeed would it have been proper for a Roman to allow that to happen. In the end, one can say that Pilate was not too afraid of Jesus to mock him.

Furious at finding himself maneuvered into a corner, Pilate struck back in angry words: "Look at your king!" The implication was that the sorry-looking specimen was alone fit to represent them. The sarcasm was plain, and bit deep. The reaction was swift; they shouted demands that this man be taken away and crucified. Pilate asked, "Shall I crucify your king?" The question drew from the chief priests, the official spokesmen of the people, the solemn reply "We have no king but Caesar" (Jn 19:16).

These words are an admission that the Roman Emperor had now become their king. This was something never before conceded even for an instant by any Jew. For Israel there was only one true king—Yahweh. Israel's claim to glory was that God alone was the true head of the chosen People.

Were the words of the highpriests a renunciation of Israel's messianic hopes, and abandonment of the faith by which the nation lived? Hardly that. It is not possible to believe that these men were speaking for all the Jews of Jerusalem or for the "scattered ones" of the Diaspora. They spoke for themselves. For them, the kingdom of the world was preferable to the kingdom of God.

The Condemnation

Perceiving that he was getting nowhere, and that the growing excitement of the crowd could easily explode into violence, Pilate motioned for a basin and water, and washed his hands in sight of all. He declared, " 'I am innocent of this righteous man's blood. See to it yourselves.' At this, the whole people cried out, 'His blood be on us and on our children' " (Mt 27:24–25). Handwashing as a symbolic gesture of disavowal is known to Romans, Greeks, Jews, and even in the West. Formal sentence was then pronounced, irrevocable except by an appeal to the Emperor. The words were simple: *Ibis ad crucem* ("You shall go to the cross"), or *Arbori infelici suspendito* ("You are to be hung upon the unlucky tree").

Only the Fourth Gospel explicitly mentions the place of

judgment, the day, and the hour of Christ's judgment. Pilate handed Jesus over to be crucified at "about the sixth hour" (19:14). (Mark says they crucified him at "the third hour." Noon was the time when the third hour ended and the sixth hour began. Thus we surmise that noon was the decisive moment.) Around noon, on the day of preparation for the Passover, Jesus was led from the Praetorium, bearing his cross, to begin the slow, painful journey to Calvary, and to death.

CHAPTER EIGHT

The Crucifixion

John carefully notes that Jesus went out carrying his cross. This was customary practice. The victim was obliged to carry the crossbeam or patibulum to the place of execution. But laws yield to physical circumstances. Since Jesus was by this time close to exhaustion and unequal to the task—the heavy crossbeam would weigh in the neighborhood of seventy-five pounds—a certain Simon from Cyrene was singled out from the crowd and made to carry the cross for Jesus. Simon had merely been coming in to the city from the country, and his plans were unexpectedly, and surely unpleasantly, upset. He has thus become a symbol for many who, through unforeseen circumstance, come into contact with persons or truths which change their lives. It has been thought probable that this Simon, who was the father of the Alexander and Rufus mentioned by Mark (15:21), received the gift of faith and was amply rewarded for the help he gave to Jesus.

Luke mentions the large crowd that followed Jesus to Calvary. The detail is altogether probable, given man's fascination with the shedding of blood and with death. No doubt some in the crowd were Jesus' friends, but there would have been many soldiers, interested enemies, and complete strangers. Among this last group were a number of women who voiced their sympathy for the victim in the street. The Talmud speaks of the women of Jerusalem who used to prepare a drugged wine for those who were condemned to crucifixion (Mk 15:23).

Jesus halted, and spoke to these women (the ancient peoples allowed those about to die to speak) and his words were brief and to the point, and as always, surprising. "Daughters of Jerusalem, do not weep for me, but weep for yourselves and for your children. . . If they do these things when the wood is green, what will happen when it is dry?" (Lk 23:28–31). The innocent Jesus was the "green wood," and those responsible for his death were the dry wood, and divine justice would be the more severe on those who deserved it. "If the righteous [man] is requited on earth, how much more the wicked and the sinner!" (Prv 11:31; 1 Pt 4:18). In these few words of Jesus, always so full of goodness, there is a terrible menace. This scene, however, does great honor to womankind. It may have been the women Jesus encountered on the way to Calvary who supplied Luke with some of his information. Luke is the *scriba mansuetudinis Christi*, the scribe of Jesus' kindness. Jesus' mercy is stressed in Luke's gospel, especially in his passion account.

The Two Thieves

Luke alone mentions the two thieves who were Jesus' companions on the march to Calvary (23:32). It is hardly likely that the Romans intended further to humiliate the condemned Jesus by crucifying him with thieves. A more likely explanation is that by their executing three criminals at once, they avoided making crucifixion a common sight. They wished to preserve its shock value.

The Crucifixion

Jesus was led outside of the city to a place called Golgotha, or in Latin, Calvary. The word signifies a skull, and referred no doubt to the peculiar shape of the terrain. The crucifixion itself is described in the simplest possible terms; the evangelists make no attempt to heighten the gory details. Eastern in origin, crucifixion traces back to the Phoenicians, from whom it had passed to many nations. The Romans reserved crucifixion as a punishment for slaves, or criminals of the lowest type. It was deemed incompatible with the dignity of Roman citizens, who could only be put to death by the sword.

Shapes of crosses varied. Sometimes the cross was a single stake, sometimes two diagonal pieces of wood; at other times a crossbeam might be set upon a fixed upright piece, either at the very top (thus forming a T or Tau cross), or a little down from the top (our familiar cross). In the West, it has become customary to picture Jesus upon a cross with the beam down from the top because a title was fixed over his head (Mt 27:37). However, room for a title could just as easily be found on a T-type cross.

The place of execution was outside, but near the city (Heb 13:12; Jn 19:20). It was near the road, so that passersby could see that Roman authority was not to be trifled with (Mk 15:29). Upon arrival, the condemned man was stripped of his clothing. Thrown to the ground, the crossbeam thrust under his shoulders, his hands were tied or nailed to the ends of the cross. The crossbeam was then raised and fitted into, or attached to the upright, which may have been permanently fixed in place. Jutting out from the upright there was sometimes a peg upon which the victim's crotch would rest, but no ancient writer mentions a footrest upon which the weight would be borne. The victim's knees were bent to the necessary angle, and the feet fastened singly, flat, to the upright. In all, four nails were probably used.

The one lingering touch of humanity in this barbarous business was the cup of wine mixed with myrrh offered to the victims; it acted as a type of sedative. Jesus went to his death with unclouded consciousness, but he acknowledged the offer by touching the drink with his lips (Mt 27:34).

In crucifixion, death often came slowly. The nails were driven into the hands and feet at a point where they would aggravate the median nerve, and the weight of the victim upon this nerve insured an unremitting and constant barrage of pain. The position of the arms made it impossible to breathe properly, and the carbon dioxide could not be exhaled efficiently from the lungs. Thus the victim's breathing would grow more and more shallow, and he would experience the sensation of asphyxiation. Panic would then drive the victim to push and pull upon his feet and hands to gain an upright position and a proper breath, paying a terrible price in pain for it. It was with such dearly purchased breath that Jesus uttered his words from the Cross. Three hours later, or the "ninth hour," Pilate's soldiers found that they did not have to break Jesus' legs to insure his death. He had already died, at about 3 p.m.

The Title on the Cross

The reason for a criminal's condemnation to the cross was written on a placard which was carried before him on the way to the site of execution, or simply hung about his neck. All four gospels record the inscription placed upon Jesus' cross. It was written in the three languages of the empire, religion, and intellect—Latin, Hebrew-Aramaic, and Greek. It is odd that the exact wording has not been preserved. The title proclaimed Jesus of Nazareth to be the King of the Jews. To Mark's brief "The King of the Jews," Matthew and John add the name "Jesus," and John gives his place of origin, "Nazareth." Our familiar I.N.R.I. stands for the Latin: *Iesus Nazarenus Rex Iudaeorum.*

Occasions such as this evoke strange reactions from people. The Synoptics record that the bystanders jeered at the victim and derisively invited him to save himself, to come down from the cross and thus prove himself (Mt 27:39–43). Joining in the insults were the highpriests and the scribes, as well as the two thieves who had been crucified with Jesus.

It was probably not long before the pagans in the crowd tired of taunting a victim who paid no attention to their jibes, so they turned to mock the Jews whose "king" was crucified before them. Tender sensibilities quickly stung, the chief priests led a delegation to Pilate, protesting that Pilate should not have identified Jesus as "King of the Jews." But Pilate was finally firm. He may not have worded the title on the cross as he did in order to annoy the priests, but surely he had simply stated the reason *they* had charged against the victim. He would not change a word of it.

God's ways are nowhere more mysterious than they are on

Calvary. The Christian, gazing upon the spectacle of Christ dying, sees him vindicated in that very moment. The picture becomes reality, and the king enters his kingdom.

The Division of Garments

The Synoptics record that lots were cast over Jesus' garments, without indicating that this act was a fulfillment of a prophecy (Ps 22:19). Four soldiers divided the garments in four ways. However, one garment was Jesus' seamless tunic, woven from top to bottom. It would have lost its value if cut up into smaller pieces. Possibly the tunic was given to Jesus by one of his followers. Fanciful speculations (it was miraculously woven, or woven by his mother Mary) impress no one today. Since the time of St. Cyprian, the Fathers have considered the tunic as a symbol of the Church and of the indestructible unity of the Church.

Some wonder if Jesus was subject to the ultimate indignity of being crucified naked. This is of course possible, but all depictions of the crucifixion show the victim covered across the middle.

CHAPTER NINE

The Seven Last Words

BEGIN

At unexpected intervals, on Calvary, Jesus raised his voice and spoke. Each of his utterances has come to be known as a "word." First there was a word of extraordinary generosity, a prayer for his executioners. This was followed by a magnificent promise made to a fellow sufferer, the repentant thief. A third word confided his beloved mother to the care of the beloved disciple. Then, as his sufferings grew more acute, Jesus cried out in the growing darkness, a strange haunting cry: "My God, my God! Why have you forsaken me?" Next, a word that revealed a raging thirst. After that, the dramatic declaration that all was finished, and finally, he commended his soul into his Father's hands. Each word calls for our devout attention.

"Father, forgive them;
they do not know what they do."

The first word is a revelation of the tender heart of Jesus. It comes as no surprise that this word appears in the third gospel (Lk 23:34), which so frequently stresses the mercy and forgiveness of God, and of the Savior. Jesus probably uttered this first prayer as his hands were being nailed to the crosspiece. This nailing was more conveniently done on the ground; once the crosspiece was fitted to the upright (which remained standing), the feet of the victim could easily be nailed.

Jesus addressed his Father, not as God and Lord, but under

the endearing title of Father. He was asking for forgiveness, not for judgment. His words applied not so much to the soldiers who were merely carrying out orders, as to those responsible for his death, namely, the religious leaders of the people. These men had closed their eyes to the signs Jesus had given, and had acted out of envy and hatred. The ordinary people were much less well-informed than their leaders, and ignorance certainly diminished their guilt in the eyes of God. Like many after them, the people had been prompted by zeal without knowledge.

Under the Old Law, the *lex talionis*, that is, an eye for an eye, a tooth for a tooth, had prevailed. Jesus had often spoken of the need to be forgiving, and had provoked the astonished question: How often must I forgive my brother if he wrongs me? Seven times? To Peter's question, Jesus replied, "Not seven times, but seventy times seven" (Mt 18:20). Here, then, Jesus gives a tremendous example of forgiveness. He renounced the claims of rigorous justice. He really meant it when he taught: "Love your enemies, and pray for those who persecute you" (Mt 5:44).

This first word of Jesus is thrilling, profound, divine, and most importantly, human. It can be imitated. In comparison to it, how shallow, cold, and brittle is our modern idolatry of science and contempt for the unlearned! And even more chilling is our modern rugged individualism, which has been given expression in a parody of Jesus' words: "Father, forgive me, for I know not what I am doing. And please don't tell me!"

"I assure you, this day you will be with me in Paradise."

Normally, a place of execution is not a place for lofty sentiments. The crowd and the magistrates who gathered to stare at the three victims on their crosses saw them as objects of legitimate scorn and ridicule. Jesus was flanked by two thieves to whom non-biblical tradition has given the names of Dismas and Gestas. Somehow, Jesus was singled out as the special target of the mockery: He saved others; let him save himself if he is the Messiah of God, his Chosen One. Even the soldiers joined in this verbal abuse: "If you are the king of the Jews, save yourself" (Lk 23:35–37). The two robbers who were crucified with him also reproached him (Mt 27:44).

Then something unexpected occurred, as it so often does where Jesus is involved. On Calvary, he was destined to die upon his cross. In the eyes of many present there, he was a failure; his career had come to a dismal end. Yet there was something about him that struck one of the thieves. This innocent man, he thought, would be a king in spite of everything. Dismas (as some name him) was probably thinking that Jesus would be crowned Messiah at the resurrection of the dead at the end of time. He asked: "Jesus, remember me when you come in your kingly power." It was a short prayer, but a good one.

Jesus had nothing to say to those who mocked him on the cross, but in answer to this touching prayer, he replied in words that have never been forgotten: "Truly I say to you, this day you will be with me in Paradise" (Lk 23:43). The Persian word "paradise" is used three times in the Bible, referring to a garden filled with trees and delight, a place of happiness. On Jesus' lips the word had another meaning, namely, wherever it is that souls go after death. Thus at the moment of his death, the good thief will find himself to be with Jesus. As Ambrose put it: "To be with Christ is life." Wherever Christ is, there is life, and his kingdom.

Jesus' second word from the cross has enveloped the world in an immense compassion. So great is the love of God for man that even a life of sin can end in sudden glory.

" 'Woman, there is your son.' Then he said to the disciple: 'Behold, your mother!' "

The word "woman" is not pejorative but a respectful term, as at Cana and at the empty tomb (Jn 2:4; 20:15). Jesus' mother was so addressed. She was standing near the cross, accompanied by three others: an unnamed sister, Mary Clopas, and

Mary Magdalene. At first the Roman guard and the enemies of Christ kept the crowd back, to make sure that the victim did not escape or be rescued by his followers. As their vigilance relaxed, the women drew closer to the crucified victim. He then spoke to his mother and the disciple John (Jn 19:25–27). The third word is one of pathos and of command. Jesus was sensitive to the plight of his mother and commended her to one whom he loved, the Disciple. His earthly existence had begun with Mary's consent and in her womb; the last words recorded of that existence concerned his mother. John accepted the charge laid upon him, for "from that hour the disciple took her to his own home," probably in Jerusalem (Acts 1:14). Epiphanius does not definitely state that Mary accompanied John to Ephesus, and a fifth century tradition locates her tomb in the Kedron valley just north of the garden of Gethsemani. A later tradition (seventh century) fixes the place of her death on the west side of Jerusalem, where the Benedictine church of the Dormition now stands.

The literal meaning of Jesus' words is simply this: Mary was to be a mother to John, and he in turn was to provide her with food and shelter. One might with some reason argue from this fact that Jesus was an only child. Roman Catholic piety toward the Blessed Virgin Mary, Mother of God, is disturbing to many, yet this side of Catholicism rests upon solid biblical and theological foundations. "When the fulness of time came, God sent his Son, *born of a woman.* . . . that we might receive the adoption of sons" (Gal 4:4–5). Her position rests squarely on Christ; he alone is the "Mediator between God and man" (1 Tm 2:5), and she who assented to become his mother also accepted a relationship with all who would fall under the influence of the Redeemer. It is a characteristic of Christ's redemptive grace that it raises men to a share in his being and his activity. A grace received from him becomes a source of salvation for one's fellows. This holds true in a special way of Mary; she who received into herself the source of all life, becomes the spiritual mother of all other members of Christ. She was the new Eve who offered her Son on Golgotha, together with the sacrifice of her maternal rights and love.

Mary's complete and utter subordination to Jesus is beautifully expressed in her instructions to the servants at the wedding feast at Cana (Jn 2:5). The words sum up her role in life and in God's saving plan: "Do whatever he tells you."

Mary was intimately connected with Jesus' work historically, objectively, and existentially. She was not on a level with Christ, for she was a creature like everyone else, but she was redeemed in a more sublime manner. Her relationship with him carried beyond history but on a higher plane. In other words, at death, one's history passes with him into God's presence. Mary's sharing in the redemptive work of Christ continues. She is present before the Father with a mother's concern for her Son's brothers and sisters on earth, only she does not walk in the obscurity of faith, as she did while on earth.

"My God, my God! Why have you forsaken me?"

The darkness of Calvary, lasting from the sixth to the ninth hour, is mentioned by all three Synoptics (Mt 27:45). This would correspond roughly to our 12:00–3:00 p.m. As the moon was at the full (it was Passover time), the darkness cannot be explained by an eclipse of the sun, but it may have been produced by a heavy cloud-bank which blotted out the sun. When the Khamsin or black sirocco moves in on Jerusalem from the southwest, as it does each Spring, a deep pall falls over the land. Possibly the gospel darkness was something like that. But it seems that nature itself was protesting the sufferings inflicted upon Jesus.

Only Matthew (27:46) and Mark (15:34) have preserved Jesus' lament, "My God, my God! Why have you forsaken me?" It is a disturbing cry, not the kind of saying one would invent for one's hero. The first two evangelists record it without comment; they apparently did not feel the words to be incompatible with Jesus' divinity. But Luke and John both omit this cry, and many after them have found it difficult to understand how Jesus, whose delight it had always been to do the will of his Father in heaven, could give voice to such a cry. The Arians and the Nestorians, early heretics, found in these words a reason for holding that Jesus was a mere man. He had perhaps dreamed of being the Messiah, but on the cross that illusion was shattered, and there he was forced to realize that God was no longer with him. Hence his great cry of abandonment.

The dereliction of Jesus on the cross poses many difficult theological problems touching upon the central mystery of the Christian faith. Did Jesus know who he was? Was he aware of the significance of his death? What do these words mean? Could he be abandoned and not abandoned, blissfully happy and profoundly suffering at the same time? ⅃—↘ P. /28

In this area, where even angelic theologians advance with caution, St. Thomas, the prince of theologians, has blazed a path into the mystery. He discusses the fourth "word" in the *Summa* (3a, q.46, aa.7–8).

Suffering. This world is, as is evident to everyone, a vale of tears. Suffering never leaves man's side for long. For some, this is a tragic side to human living, clay on man's wings, so to speak. St. Thomas was not by nature given to simplistic views, and he penetrated the mystery of suffering. It is sometimes punitive, sometimes medicinal, but always an opportunity to walk with Jesus, whose expiatory sufferings brought healing and peace to the world. Jesus is the supreme example of unselfish love, and the spectacle of the Savior kneeling in blood-drenched garments, or stretched out upon the cross in extraordinary pain, has touched the hearts of saints and sinners in every age. Physical pain is only part of the picture, of course; Jesus suffered inwardly also, for he knew the bitterness of betrayal, disloyalty, contempt, and (and here the mystery becomes most profound) abandonment by God.

Bliss. Happiness is the pleasant result of the conscious realization that one is in possession of a desired good. Tidings of good fortune induce people to jump and dance for joy. As God's beloved Son, Jesus rejoiced with God in the divine nature, and theologians have not hesitated to conclude that even in his humanity, Jesus saw the face of his heavenly Father, and rejoiced at that blessed vision.

On the other hand, the gospels provide the Arians and their

modern counterparts, the humanists, with plenty of ammunition. Much is said about Jesus' emotional life in the gospels. He wept over Jerusalem and shed tears at the tomb of his friend Lazarus. He found the slowness of the disciples frustrating, and their bumbling attempts to "steer" him (Mt 16:22; Mk 10:14) aroused his indignation. His public career was, after the honeymoon period in Galilee, one long series of running battles and public debates with the members of the establishment. On more than one occasion his words were sharp and cutting. Nor was it just his words: there was one unforgettable day when his anger exploded and he literally drove the buyers and sellers out of the Temple. François Mauriac even wrote a book about the angry Christ.

While, then, there is no great evidence that Jesus enjoyed the bliss of heaven during his earthly life, nor any of its secondary effects, a case can be made out that he did. His walking upon the waters would be some proof that his body obeyed other laws than those of the mass of humanity, and his transfiguration on Mount Thabor was a brief manifestation of the glory that was within. St. Thomas argued that the "head" of the body ought to have all the perfections that any of his "members" would have, but in a more excellent way.

Simultaneous suffering and bliss. A skillful debater can, by stressing certain details and ignoring others, make his side of the case appear to be clearly conclusive. In an earlier age, some so stressed Jesus' divinity that his humanity appeared to be a mere shell. Today the emphasis is the other way around: his humanity is over-stressed. The Church's assurance that Jesus was and is also both God and Man sheds a steady light on his sufferings, death, and resurrection—that is, on the mystery of the Incarnation. In this light, the theologians persist in their attempts to understand who and what Jesus was. They may experiment with philosophical terms which cannot be verified, chapter and verse, in the Bible, but such terms retain their own validity, and in the proper hands, become tools whereby we seek to "know the love of Christ which is beyond all knowledge" (Eph 3:18). Let this one example suffice.

Where Jesus is concerned, the one-to-one relationship (that

is, *one nature* going with *one person* to constitute *a human being*) simply does not apply. As has frequently been said, Jesus will not fit into any of our manmade categories. He presents us with the unique and unforeseen spectacle of two natures, one human and the other divine, united in one single divine person. Each nature was, so to speak, "protected" from the other. Thanks to his human nature, he had like ourselves a body and soul, intellect and will and all the senses. In every way he was a true human being, except that his center of attribution, his "I" was the "I" of God. He was different; he is unique. He was, as Aquinas says, in his human nature both a seer of God (a *comprehensor*) and a wayfarer (a *viator*).

The solution of the problem of Jesus' dereliction on the cross must be sought in the light of that brief statement. While enduring atrocious sufferings, Jesus "knew in the depths of his being that he was personally bound to his Father in love." He experienced the estrangement from God that belongs to our sinfulness; he identified himself with the alienation from God that sin produces. He had to pass through the helplessness of that alienation from God to receive the glory which the Father had in store for him.* The protection which the Father had maintained over his Son up to now was temporarily suspended. Christ redeemed us from the curse of the Law by being cursed for our sake, Paul says (Gal 3:13). "He who knew no sin was 'made sin' for our sakes" (2 Cor 5:21).

To sum up, then, Jesus, truly man and the natural Son of God, knew full well who he was. No evangelist invented him or his claims or his teachings. Secondly, he was surely aware of the significance of his sufferings and death, both being willed by his Father as part of the divine plan for man's salvation.

The explanation for the fourth "word" lies in this understanding of God's plan in Jesus. "My God, My God, Why have you forsaken me" is the beginning of Psalm 22, a psalm that ends in a cry of triumph and joy. On Jesus' lips, "My God" is an affirmation of faith, a prayer that reflected his inner feel-

---

*E. Schillebeeckx, *Christ the Sacrament*, p.27

ings. More than any man that ever lived, he experienced the darkness and distress of death, for at the moment God was for him, as Kasper writes, the one who is totally other, who "withdraws in his very closeness." The extremity of Jesus' emptiness made it possible for him to become the vessel of God's fullness, and his death became the source of life; it was the final revelation of the only thing he was interested in, the coming of God's eschatological rule. In it we see a compound of human powerlessness, wealth in poverty, love in desolation, abundance in emptiness, and life in death.*

The fourth "word" makes it clear to all sinners that man was not redeemed cheaply, but at great cost. Jesus' patient endurance up to this point might have led some to suppose that he had no feelings. His cry of abandonment disproves that. Calvary teaches much about the malice of sin, the holiness of God, and the mystery of God's love (Rom 5:6–16).

"I Thirst"

Jesus' ministry to others was now finished, and this fifth word bears witness to his own sufferings. He had not had anything to drink since the wine at the Last Supper. The bloody sweat in the garden would alone account for a drastic lowering of his vitality, and in addition to that he had undergone the exhausting interrogations of the trail, had been moved about (from the pretorium to Herod's and back), had been painfully scourged, and borne his cross to Calvary, and had undergone the torments of crucifixion. His thirst was unquestionably great.

John introduced the fifth "word" with the thought-provoking statement that Jesus "knowing that all was now finished, said 'I thirst,' to fulfill the scriptures" (19:28). Two texts come immediately to mind: "For my thirst they gave me vinegar to drink" (Ps 69:22) and "My soul thirsts for God, for the living God" (Ps 42:2). All that the Father had sent the Son to do had been carried out; the gospels tell us that. But that Son had an

---

*W. Kasper, *Jesus the Christ*, p.118–19.

important pronouncement to make, and to do that clearly he had first to moisten his lips.⌐

Someone, probably one of the soldiers, moistened a sponge with the thin, dry wine which soldiers were permitted to bring with them on duty. With a touch of rough kindness he raised it to Jesus' lips "on hyssop." Hyssop is a small bush that has blue flowers and highly aromatic leaves. The hyssop stem is short and pliant, and unless several of them had been tied together, it could not have raised a wine-soaked sponge very high. The crosses were from eight to ten feet in height, much too high for the pliant hyssop. The text is unusually well-attested, and it is unlikely that *hyssopo* is a mistake for *hysso* (spear or javelin), the reading adopted by some.

It has been suggested that since hyssop was used to smear the blood of the passover lamb on the doorposts of the Jews in Egypt as a sign of God's protection (Ex 12:22), that the text was deliberately altered from *hysso* (javelin) to *hyssopo* (hyssop). Jesus was both the lamb of God (Jn 1:33) and the door of the sheepfold (10:7), and the soldier's act may have been intended to remind readers that the Passover was being fulfilled once and for all in the sacrifice of Jesus, the true Paschal lamb. But this is rather subtle, and not wholly accurate. John's text speaks of a sponge on hyssop, but not at all that the hyssop was being used as a life-giving sponge. Matthew (27:48) and Mark (15:36) have the soldier using a reed, not hyssop.

"It Is Finished"

Jesus concluded his life as a writer ends his book by saying: this is the end. But in Jesus' case the words had layers of meaning. He had completed the work for which he had been sent, had broken the bonds of sin, and so, fittingly and triumphantly, cried out "It is finished!" (Jn 19:30). The significance of his cry did not escape the Byzantine artists who portrayed Jesus on the cross garbed in robes of royalty. From a human point of view, the words must also have been invested with relief and satisfaction. The perfect sacrifice was now offered. He could die.

"Father, Into Your Hands, I Commit My Spirit"

Even in death, Jesus was surprising. The evangelists all use unusual ways to describe that death. They do not say that he died, but that he "breathed his last" (Mark, Luke), "yielded" (Matthew) or "gave up his spirit" (John). Luke explains that Jesus addressed his Father "with a loud cry" (Lk 23:46), with an outburst of energy that seemed to defy his human condition. It is by no means fantastic to speak of Jesus' voluntary death. The gospels record that he once said, "For this reason the Father loves me, because I lay down my life that I may take it again. No one takes it from me, but I lay it down of my own accord. I have power to lay it down, and I have power to take it again" (Jn 10:17-18). What he is saying is that his soul would not quit his body unless he gave it permission to depart. An astounding claim, but here was no ordinary man. His soul, besides being perfectly human, was the conjoined instrument of divinity, and endowed with a power coextensive with that of the agent who directed it, that is, with God himself. Jesus' death could then be, and was, miraculously controlled. But the miraculous seems almost natural in the life of Jesus of Nazareth.

If Jesus died only when he wished to die, it is reasonable to ask why he wanted to die at all. The unexpected answer is provided in the gospel: "This charge I have received from my Father" (Jn 9:18). Jesus had received a command from his Father to lay down his life. We have Jesus' own assurance of this. In carrying out the command first uttered in the unfathomable and eternal life of the Trinity, Jesus also fulfilled all the commands which God had ever given to men in the Old Law: the moral precepts (by his love and obedience), the ceremonial precepts (in his own death, which was that of a perfect victim, all the sacrifices of the Old Law were summed up and brought to perfection), and the judicial commands (his atoning death more than sufficiently satisfied the claim of justice).

What was the Father like, thus to deliver his well-beloved Son to death? A loving God, of course. "He who does not love does not know God; for God is love" (1 Jn 4:8). God who is love sent his only begotten Son into the world that men might live through him. "In this is love, not that we loved God but that he loved us and sent his Son to be the expiation of our sins" (1 Jn 4:10). Paul sounded the same note when he wrote: "While we were enemies we were reconciled to God by the death of his Son" (Rom 5:9). It was out of love that the Father handed his Son over to death, and it was out of love that Jesus died.

Jesus died, then, not of exhaustion, but because he willed it. He said "It is finished"; and he bowed his head (John noticed that) and gave up his spirit.

There is a sense in which Jesus gave up his spirit to those who stood near him at the foot of the Cross, in fulfillment, as it were, of promises he had made earlier:

> All that the Father gives me will come to me,
>   and him who comes to me I will not cast out.
> For I have come down from heaven,
>   not to do my own will, but
>   the will of him who sent me.
> Now the will of him who sent me
>   is that I should lose nothing
>   of all he has given me, but
>   that I should raise it up at the last day.
> And this is the will of my Father,
>   that every one who sees the Son and believes in him,
>   should have eternal life.
> And I will raise him up at the last day (Jn 6:37–40).

Natural Wonders

As the sound of Jesus' voice died away, a number of strange things began to happen. The colorful veil of the Temple was suddenly rent from top to bottom. It is not clear which of the two Temple veils is meant. One, called the *paroketh*, divided the Holy of Holies from the section called the Holy Place. Another, the *masok*, covered the entrance into the Temple building. The symbolism, at any rate, is clear: sinners now have access to God. Jesus' death opened the way to God; the barrier was broken down (Eph 2:14). Under the Old Law, only the high Priest could enter the Holy of Holies, and that only on the feast of Yom Kippur, the great day of expiation. Now, "the blood of Jesus assures our entrance into the sanctuary by the new and living path he has opened up for us through the veil (the "veil" meaning his flesh). . . let us draw near in . . . confidence" (Heb 10:19–22). Any man, whether Jew or Gentile, can now look at will into the Holy Place. The way to God is open.

Matthew records the earthquake which occurred at Jesus' death. "The earth shook and the rocks were split; the tombs also were opened" (27:52). Earthquakes are not uncommon in the Holy Land, the most recent one being that of 1927. These account for the many dislocated slabs over the tombs that surround Jerusalem. On Calvary itself there is a fissure which actually runs across the grain of the bedrock, close to the spot where Jesus' cross was raised. It was the quake which caused the tearing of the veils in the Temple.

Only Matthew noted that many bodies of the saints who had fallen asleep were raised. "They came forth from their tombs and entered the holy city and appeared to many" (27:52–53). Early commentators exercised their ingenuity in trying to establish the identity of these "saints." Did these dead merely stir to life and then subside? The text says that three days later they went into the city . . . strange behavior for the dead indeed! Matthew is generally more precise than this. However, the apocalyptic and eschatological overtones of the verse suggest that Matthew was using an appropriate literary form to describe what happened. The symbolism of this passage is clear: by Jesus' death and resurrection, the saints of the Old Israel join with those of the New. Matthew is also here anticipating the final act of man's history.

Bystanders

During the crucifixion, a soldier stood facing Jesus on the cross (Mt 27:54). He took in everything during the three hours Jesus hung on the cross. A centurion, he was the officer in charge of a hundred men, although only four had been detailed to this task. The centurion's name appears only in the apocryphal writings, where he is called Longinus; the name is probably a derivation of the Greek word for spear (*longche*). He is also called Petronius. He had probably seen many crucifixions, but his words, "Truly this man was the Son of God!" (Mk 15:39) reveal that he had been profoundly moved by Jesus' death, and possibly also by the natural wonders that accompanied it. His words can hardly be taken as an expression of belief in Jesus' divinity, for *huios theou* without the definite article means "a son of God." Luke captures the nuance, and has the centurion say, "Surely this was an innocent (*dikaios*) man" (Lk 23:47). There is, however, a deeper meaning in what the centurion said; he unwittingly hit upon a profound statement of the truth: Jesus *is* a Son of God, even the Son of God. For Matthew and Mark, these words form the climax of their crucifixion narratives.

Who saw Jesus die? Besides the Roman soldiers, and the priestly enemies of Jesus, there were many people. Luke mentions the crowd that had assembled for the sight of a public execution (23:48). He also says that many of these went home disturbed and thoughtful, beating their breasts. Many of Jesus' friends were there, and women representing devout women everywhere. Some of these had ministered to Jesus and his co-workers in Galilee (they must then have been wealthy), and had followed them to Jerusalem. When the Apostles fled, leaving Christ alone, the women remained. With that remarkable strength women almost always show in adversity, they stood at a distance, looking on. The first two evangelists mention their names: Mary Magdalene, Mary the mother of James and Joseph, and the mother of the sons of Zebedee. These were to share in Jesus' burial (Mk 15:47), and would bring additional gifts of spices (16:1). They would be the first to hear of the resurrection (16:5f), would continue in prayer until Pentecost (Acts 1:14), and would open their homes to Christian worship (Acts 12:12). The church is deeply endebted to the *pia feminea sexus* (the pious feminine sex).

The Piercing of Jesus' Side

By Jewish law, the bodies of criminals had to be removed from the cross before nightfall. Of course they had to die first. On this occasion, it was doubly important that the victims die soon because at dusk both the sabbath and the Passover feast began. The Jews did not want to have the bodies left on the cross during the sabbath, especially as that sabbath was a solemn feast day (Jn 19:31). A delegation therefore called on the procurator, who was at his residence (Pilate had not personally overseen the crucifixion), and asked that the legs of the crucified be broken, thus hastening their death by asphyxiation. This barbarous practice of breaking legs by blows with a heavy maul was known as the *crurifragium*. Originally it was a separate form of capital punishment, comparable in some respects to that of the wheel. Pilate agreed.

When the soldiers came to Jesus, they found that he was already dead, and so they did not break his legs. One of them, however, for no apparent reason, plunged his two-edged spear into Jesus' side, with surprising results. Immediately there flowed out blood and water. Physicians have looked into this event with professional eyes and vouch for its credibility. Heavy blows upon the chest wall can produce internal bleeding in the lung cavity, making breathing extremely difficult. Other causes might produce a similar condition. Jesus' insatiable thirst, and the bodily immobility imposed by crucifixion, would lead to an acute dilation of the stomach, of the blood vessels, arteries, and veins. Since the blood could not flow off or be quickly absorbed, it would separate into layers of plasma and red cells, a stable mixture which does not coagulate. Assuming that the soldier's lance penetrated the rib cage from below, it would be first the red blood, then the plasma, or water, that drained off.

For John, who describes this event, the piercing of Jesus' side was irrefutable proof of Jesus' death. When Jesus' body was pierced, it bled as human bodies bleed; he was no phantom man. John, however, had something else in mind in draw-

ing attention to this; the passage is heavy with spiritual significance. First, there is the unconscious fulfillment of a prophecy,
"You shall not break a bone of it [the paschal lamb's]" (Ex
12:46), and "They shall look on him whom they have pierced"
(Zec 12:10). For a Semite, blood was very special. The life of the
flesh is in the blood (Lv 17:11). Life and blood are almost interchangeable terms. Blood is not only sacred, it is a means par-
excellence of propitiating the deity. The shedding of Jesus' own
precious blood was the magnificent fulfillment of all sacrifice;
he was the perfect Paschal Lamb. His blood was and is a re-
deeming blood. Those washed in it are made clean. Without
the shedding of blood there is no forgiveness (Heb 9:22); with
this blood there is salvation.

But then, water is also a symbol of purification, and of the
new spiritual life made possible by baptism. Jesus spoke of
life-giving water to the Samaritan woman (Jn 4:14); he could
give a water that would be an inner spring welling up to
eternal life, for water seeks its own level. At the feast of
Tabernacles he declared "If anyone is thirsty, let him come to
me!" (7:37). The blood and the water flowing from Jesus' side
were two instruments of purification, and also speak to us of
the Eucharist and of Baptism. Augustine pursued the symbolism further and saw in this incident the Church issuing from
the side of the sleeping Christ, just as Eve came forth from
the side of a sleeping Adam. John would later on write,
"There are three witnesses, the Spirit, the water and the
blood" (1 Jn 5:7–8).

These rich symbols have many layers of meaning, and the
faithful have not failed to probe them. The popular devotion to
the Sacred Heart of Jesus directs our attention to the wounded
heart of him who has so loved us. Augustine is worth quoting
once again, for he often saw what ordinary men might miss.
Quid isto vulnere salubrius? he asked. "What wound was ever
more health-giving?"

Two powerful personalities stand at the beginning, and at
the end, of the Fourth Gospel, John the Baptizer and John the

Evangelist. The first cried, "Behold, the Lamb of God who takes away the sin of the world" (Jn 1:29); the second declared that "his testimony is true, and he knows that he tells the truth, that you also may believe" (Jn 19:35).

The Suffering Servant has turned out to be the Lamb of God, a Savior by his blood, and the giver of new spiritual life through the waters of Baptism.

CHAPTER TEN

The Burial

Roman law forbade the burial of the bodies of criminals who had died by crucifixion. Their bodies were to be left hanging upon the cross, legitimate prey for jackals and vultures. However, Jewish law called for the removal of such bodies by nightfall (Dt 21:23), and Jesus' friends moved into action. A man who had been a secret disciple of Jesus (Mt 27:57; Jn 12:42) went to Pilate and asked to be allowed to bury the body. He was Joseph of Arimathea, a member of the Sanhedrin (obviously then its decision had not been unanimous), and a wealthy man looking for the reign of God (Mk 15:43). Such a distinguished man could do things the apostles could not do. He went boldly in to the procurator, and asked permission to take Jesus' body.

Mark's account of this incident brings us into contact with administrative reality (15:42–47). Pilate was surprised to learn that Jesus had died, for crucifixion was a slow death, and some remained alive on the cross for two or three days. So he first sent for the centurion in charge and ascertained that Jesus was in fact dead. He then granted the body to Joseph. It was an act of courtesy or favor on Pilate's part. Relatives were sometimes allowed to ransom the bodies of their dead and give them decent burial.

Joseph and his servants were soon joined by Nicodemus. They took Jesus' body, washed and anointed it, and then wrapped it in a clean cloth which Joseph had purchased. John notes that "they took the body of Jesus and wrapped it, with the spices, in strips of linen cloth according to Jewish burial customs" (19:40). The body was swathed, then, in narrow bands which were sprinkled with a mixture of myrrh and aloes. Myrrh is a resinous gum; when used for burials it was crushed into a powder and mixed with aloes. These spices served the very practical purpose of sweetening the air about the tomb. Nicodemus had brought a hundred pounds of them. Twenty to fifty pounds were not unusual at funerals, but larger quantities were used for more important people. Herod the Great, for example, was buried beneath spices brought by five hundred slaves! (For a description of a royal funeral, see 2 Chr 16:14.)

Jesus was placed in Joseph's new, unused tomb. It was hewn out of the rock in a garden about thirty yards from Golgotha. Jerusalem has tombs everywhere, for its native limestone is relatively easy to dig. Tombs of the wealthy usually had an antechamber to the burial chambers. In these chambers, ledges or shelves ran along the walls, and the bodies were laid upon them. The remaining spices were poured over the body, and the rolling stone, large and heavy and fitting into a sleeve of rock, was allowed to fall into place, thus sealing off the opening.

Having performed this corporal act of mercy, Joseph and Nicodemus disappear from history. Their gracious deed however, is not forgotten.

> How Life and death in Thee
> Agree!
> Thou hadst a virgin womb
> and tomb.
> A Joseph did espouse
> them both.
> (Crashaw)

The Guard at the Tomb (Mt 27:62–66)

The year of Christ's death, Passover coincided with the Sabbath. On that day (here deliberately unnamed) a delegation made up of chief priests and Pharisees wended its way to the procurator's residence. During the preceding hectic days, these men had thought of many things, but not of everything. Now they recalled a disquieting fact, that this impostor, while still alive, had made the claim: "I am to be raised again after three days." It was bad enough that this man's disciples considered him to be the Messiah. If his body disappeared within the appointed time, widespread belief in his resurrection from the dead would compound the mischief. They therefore asked Pilate to post a guard over Jesus' tomb until the third day had come and gone. "Otherwise his disciples may come and steal the body and then tell the people, 'He has been raised from the dead!' " Pilate's thoughts on the matter are not recorded, but he curtly granted the permission, all the more readily as it was not uncommon to post a guard over new tombs. Roman soldiers were appointed as guards, and the usual seal was so affixed that any attempt to move the rolling stone would break it or cause it to fall to the ground.

There is no good reason for questioning the historicity of this passage. The facts are historically probable, and the Church has accepted this bit of the gospel as true. The tomb was empty after the resurrection, but not for the reason that Jesus' body had been stolen.

CHAPTER ELEVEN

The Resurrection

The Gospel Accounts

Jesus' resurrection is the heart of Christianity. It is not a belief that developed gradually in a believing community, nor an emotional experience, but an actual event that was thrust upon it. Incredulous at first, the apostles in the end accepted it as something that could not be gainsaid (1 Cor 15; Acts 2:31ff). It has been suggested that the story was invented to explain away the death of Jesus and the empty tomb, but one is impressed by witnesses who stick to their story even to the point of suffering and dying for it. And in this case the witnesses did just that.

In the reports of what happened after Jesus' death and burial, the evangelists pass over the great day of the Passover in silence; for them that feast had no further significance. The four gospels all speak of an empty tomb with surprising brevity. No attempt is made to describe what had taken place, but the apocryphal gospels make up for that with a wealth of "suitable" detail.

In contrast to the more orderly account of Jesus' Passion, the Easter story is little short of chaotic. Jesus appears and disappears in unpredictable fashion, showing himself to those who had followed and loved him, but not once to his enemies. Kaleidoscopic changes of locale occur. Many people are involved, but what is said, and by whom, and when, and where, is far from clear. The gospel accounts reflect the impact made upon the disciples by the apparently incredible news that a man had returned from the dead.

Vouched for by the unimpeachable testimony of Paul and the gospels, the resurrection has nevertheless been vigorously attacked and denied. Some fear to confront those who deny or question the resurrection, seemingly unaware of the 2000 years of Christianity's survival. Fire means light as well as heat, and the literary and historical criticism of the Bible has contributed to a deeper and more realistic understanding of that holy book. Church leaders do not share the apprehensions of some of the faithful. Pius XII's encyclical *Divino Afflante Spiritu* gave a powerful impetus to modern biblical studies (1943). The *Instruction on the Truth of the Gospels,* issued in 1964 by the Pontifical Biblical Commission on Scripture, illustrates the process whereby new knowledge is positively assimilated by the old. Vatican Council II spoke of the gospels as documents that reliably handed on the events of the human life of Jesus, that is, what he really did and taught for man's salvation. The *Dei Verbum,* a document issued by the Council in 1965, stated that under the guidance of the Holy Spirit, there had been some development of the original story; under the guidance of the Holy Spirit, the evangelists advanced in the understanding of Jesus and his works after the resurrection. Thus the "books of scripture must be acknowledged as teaching firmly, faithfully, and without error, that truth which God wanted put into the sacred writings for the sake of our salvation."

In statements like these, the new (a better understanding of how the gospels came to be written) is joined to the old (the belief that the gospels unfailingly lead us in the ways of salvation). Once again reason is not viewed as an enemy of the faith but as, rather, an important ally.

As further proof that there is to be no going back on the *Divino Afflante Spiritu,* Pope Paul VI in 1970 invited scholars from many countries to Rome, to discuss the problem of Jesus' bodily resurrection. Under this papal patronage, the scholars reached an agreement on a critical understanding of the post-resurrectional Gospel accounts. The gap between the scholar and the ordinary believer here is wide, but one that can fortunately be bridged in time by education.

One can, then, view the accounts of Jesus' resurrection and

appearances with some confidence. Eleven appearances of the risen Lord are recorded in the New Testament: to Simon Peter (Lk 24:34), to Mary Magdalene (Jn 20:11–18), to the women (Mt 28:9ff), to two disciples on the road to Emmaus (Lk 24:13–32), to the apostles with Thomas absent (Jn 20:24ff), to the apostles with Thomas present (Jn 20:26ff), to the disciples and faithful gathered together in Galilee (Jn 21:1ff), to the apostles upon a mountain (Mt 28:16), to more than 500 disciples at once (1 Cor 15:6), to James (1 Cor 15:7), and to the apostles just before the ascension (Lk 24:50–53; Mk 16:19). Finally, some years later, there was an appearance to Paul on the road to Damascus (1 Cor 15:8; Acts 9:3ff).

The accounts are not easy to reconcile. Luke puts them all on Easter day; he also omits all mention of appearances in Galilee. For him, everything came to a focus in Jerusalem. Matthew records only a brief appearance to the women, instructing them about a Galilean rendezvous. Finally, note must be taken of the fact that the gospels were written from thirty to sixty years after the event.

The loose ends which so distract the modern reader had apparently no great importance in the eyes of the apostolic men with whom the gospel originated. The gospels were written to confirm the faith of believers and those who were disposed to believe in what they had to say. The important thing, for these writers, was to proclaim the extraordinary fact that *Jesus was seen alive after his death and burial*. The gospels represent the results of a reflective process that began with Jesus' resurrection. Decades of proclamation and witness, of preaching and teaching, led to a better understanding of what Jesus himself taught and what he meant. This greater understanding is evident in many places: in Mt 28:19 for example (the formula for baptism), in Mt 28:16–20 (the mission of the Church to go to all nations, to teach them), in John 20:26 (the importance of the first day of the week).

The Empty Tomb

The number of questions that have been raised here is almost beyond counting. Was Jesus buried at all? Was he not simply thrown into a common pit reserved for criminals? Some have held this, but one cannot easily write off Joseph of Arimathea, who is mentioned in all four gospels. There is a problem whether Jesus was anointed before burial. Compare Mark and Luke to John. The role of the women and their spices after the sabbath is far from clear. As for the empty tomb, a growing number of scholars now consider that this tradition was later added to the narratives of Jesus' death and burial and resurrection. The angels at the tomb can easily be seen as "interpreters of the divine mysteries," and the empty tomb was a good connecting link between the Passion of Jesus and his appearances. But by itself, the empty tomb really says nothing about the resurrection; it has to be interpreted. Essentially, it is a negative fact, and as such has been vigorously challenged. The main arguments, now generally abandoned, are these: (1) The apostles stole the body at night. This ancient charge may reflect the Judaeo-Christian polemic, and appears in Matthew's gospel; (2) Members of the Sanhedrin (or the Romans) took the body and hid it in an unmarked grave; (3) Joseph of Arimathea at the last moment put the body in another tomb; (4) Jesus had not really died, but being marvellously fit, revived in the cool of the tomb, pushed away the stone blocking the entrance and wandered off into oblivion; (5) Magdalene in her fervid imagination simply imagined she had seen and talked with the Master and persuaded the apostles to share in her illusion.

These alternatives to Jesus' bodily resurrection are not very convincing, for they require a summary dismissal of the only available documents that deal with a belief in the resurrection. It is asking too much. The fact of Christianity rests upon the apostolic belief in the resurrection of Jesus. However difficult the interpretation of the gospel accounts may be, these constitute a large part of the New Testament, and their inspired character is vouched for by the Church. This means that the challenge, not the evidence, must crumble and give way. The word of the Lord shall abide forever.

It is one thing to recognize the gospels as a literary form employed by the evangelists both to record the faith of the early Christian community and to confirm it in that faith. But it is quite another thing to deny the historical reliability of the gospels on that account. Jesus appeared to many people after his death. If the gospels are not history in our sense of that word, they are legitimate products of the reflective process by which the Church came gradually to see what Jesus meant to her, and what he really was.

The gospels, then, are basically historical. The empty tomb is a great fact, but so is the reaction of Jesus' disciples when they saw the Lord. The original good news was just that: "We have seen the Lord!" Here we have not simply one of many articles of faith, but the central premise itself. Paul said this directly, "If Christ was not raised our faith is worthless" (1 Cor 15:14). Many things are of secondary importance—the rending of the Temple veil, the stirring of the dead in their graves, the guard at the tomb, the angel or the angels—and these may well be examples of pictorial thinking or attempts to fill out the basic truth. Such thinking is compatible with the historical truth of the gospels, being a convenient and acceptable way of proclaiming the Easter faith, behind which there sounds the triumphant proclamation: "We have seen the Lord!"

The Resurrection

The resurrection of Jesus, Christianity's most profound mystery, is also its supreme argument. It is a unique event; other men who rose from the dead—for example Lazarus—died again. Jesus rose to die no more. That he did in fact die is certain; his enemies had made sure of that. Once buried, his very tomb had been guarded by soldiers. Yet he rose on the third day. Vouched for by all four evangelists, although with much divergence in details, the fact is there, and the empty tomb is a part of history.

The Women at the Tomb

Women played a prominent but not conclusive part in the resurrection story. Once the Sabbath rest was over, they set out for Jesus' tomb. Mark and Luke noted that they were carrying spices. Joseph of Arimathea and Nicodemus had heaped a generous quantity of spices over Jesus' body, but the women wanted to add their bit as well. How they were to get into the tomb appears not to have entered their minds until they were approaching it. According to Matthew (27:60), the stone which sealed the tomb was "very great." Mark concurs (16:4). To roll back such a stone would call for levers and solid muscle; moreover, a permit was required to do so. The women had not thought of these details, nor in fact did they have to, for when they arrived, the tomb was empty.

The women had come very early in the morning, and the sun which had just risen (Mark), was shining into the tomb entrance, which faced east. On seeing the stone rolled back, the women were of course quite excited. Mary Magdalene ran with the news to Peter and the other disciple (the one Jesus loved), and broke the news to them in breathless fashion. Her artless "We don't know where they have put him!" conveyed the information that she had not been alone at the tomb.

While Magdalene was on her way to Peter and John, the other women entered the tomb, and "saw a young man sitting at the right, dressed in a white robe." Luke, who speaks of "two men in dazzling garments," says that the women were "terrified." Mark has them "bewildered and trembling," and because of their great fear, "they said nothing to anyone." However, Mark's angel gave the women something to do: "Go now and tell his disciples and Peter . . ." Evidently, then, Peter was forgiven for having denied his master.

Mark limits himself to describing Jesus' appearances in Galilee, and seems not to know of his appearances in Jerusalem. "He [Jesus] is going ahead of you to Galilee, where you will see him." Luke with his Jerusalem-oriented point of view, has the angel saying "Remember what he said to you while he was still in Galilee." The women set off to tell the news to the Eleven, and it was while they were on their way that Jesus met them. "They embraced his feet and did him homage" (Mt 28:8). Luke notes that no one was willing to believe them (24:11). In that day and age, and in that cultural milieu, the official witness was that of the men.

Magdalene told her story to Peter and John, who at once ran

(from where is not stated) to the tomb. Naturally, the younger man reached it first, but for some strange reason he did not go in until after Peter had entered it. Both men saw the linen cloths lying there, and John noted that the napkin which had been on Jesus' head was not lying with the linen cloths, but was rolled up in a place by itself. From this incidental bit of information, one might reconstruct the deliberateness with which Jesus rose from the dead. Nothing suggests a cleverly organized theft of the body.

On seeing that the stone had been removed, the tomb empty and the burial cloths neatly arranged, the disciple whom Jesus loved understood what had happened: Jesus had risen. The scriptures taught that Jesus must rise from the dead, but as they did not know that (20:9), they remained in some confusion until the risen Christ convinced them of it. His predictions of his death and resurrection (Jn 2:22; 16:16) had simply not been understood, but like his parables, had been puzzling and obscure and difficult to grasp. That may be the reason why, after Peter and John had looked into the tomb, they simply "went back to their homes."

The Great Recognition

Mary Magdalene, who had returned with Peter and John, remained outside the tomb while the two men were examining it. When they emerged, silent and preoccupied, they went off without speaking. Mary remained where she was. She would be the first to see the risen Christ. Her only thought now, however, was that someone had stolen his body, and she wept because she loved him. Eyes brimming with tears, she stooped to peer into the tomb (the entrances were always low), and "saw two angels sitting" where Jesus' body had rested. So great was her sorrow that as she looked she hardly noticed the splendor of the visitors until they spoke to her: "Woman, why are you weeping?" Mechanically she replied, "Because they have taken away my Lord" (a bold possessiveness!) "and I do not know where they have laid him" (Jn 20:13f).

Uninterested in prolonging a conversation that seemed pointless, Mary turned from the tomb, and as she did, "saw

Jesus standing. But she did not know that it was Jesus." In his new state, Jesus could apparently appear or not as he willed. John Chrysostom thought it thoughtful of Christ to spare Mary the shock of a sudden confrontation. "Woman, why are you weeping?" he asked. "Whom do you seek?" Mistaking him for the gardener (for this incident occurred in a garden), she hardly glanced at him. "Sir, if you have carried him away, tell me . . . and I will take him away." She asked only to be told where *he* was, so that *she* could take him away. Clearly, she was quite distracted by her grief, and she turned away.

At this moment the Good Shepherd had only to call his beloved lamb and say "Mary," and she recognized him. She turned to him, casting herself at his feet and grasping them. She could only say, and probably did so over and over, "Rabboni" or "Teacher." Once before, Jesus had commended this woman for what she had done at a banquet; now he said "Do not hold me."

There can be little doubt that Mary Magdalene had fallen at Jesus' feet (Bernini's sculpture in SS. Giovanni e Sisto in Rome has beautifully captured the rapture of that moment) and embraced them, manifesting thus the strength and the weakness of her love. She knew it was he, but was she perhaps not assuming that he had simply returned to a mortal, earthly life in which things would go on as they had before? How could she have known at this time that Jesus had entered into a condition of life that was radically new, one that preserved but surpassed the present human condition. Thomas would be more astute, confessing Jesus' divinity. To Mary, Jesus explained why she should not hold him, "For I have not yet ascended to the Father."

Here this touching story takes on theological implications. Jesus seemed to be saying that he could be clung to, not now, but later, after his ascension to the Father. In that case he may have been saying that believers would be able to grasp and cling to him in the intimacy of faith, for faith is a kind of touching. However, it could also mean that Mary was not to remain at his feet, but was to carry a message to his brothers. The message was simply this, that Jesus "had not yet ascended [visibly] to my Father and your Father, to my God and your God."

Christ had, however, already gone to the Father and had already been given all power, and had become Lord of the Spirit. At the moment of his death, his soul went, as we say, down into hell, or the abode of the dead. At the moment of his resurrection, Jesus found himself instantly in the presence of God his Father. At that moment the human nature which the Word had assumed into a personal union was fully penetrated by the Spirit, and Jesus Christ was exalted as Lord of all creation. His human nature was glorified. This was the completion of the resurrection, the finishing touch, but not the end of the story. The crucifixion and the resurrection are different aspects of God's great saving act, but so also are the ascension and Pentecost.] E N D

Before the day was over, to judge by the gospel accounts, Jesus' actions and words would reveal that he was already completely glorified. It follows that he had already ascended to his Father.

By her commission to bear a message to the apostles, Mary became an apostle to the apostles. Her message contained a novelty: Hitherto, Jesus had referred to his disciples as "friends"; now they are "his brothers." It is interesting to note the careful distinction he makes between *My* and *Your* Father. "I am ascending to my Father and your Father, to my God and your God" (Jn 20:18). Theologians conclude from this that Jesus is the natural and eternal Son of God, whereas all his disciples have become God's adopted sons by grace.

Mary went to the disciples and reported what she had heard. Her statement, "I have seen the Lord," seems to have fallen into a void: there is no comment about the apostles' reaction.

The Guards and the Chief Priests

As the women who had come to the tomb were leaving the garden, the soldiers who had been assigned to guard the tomb were hurrying into the city, and some of them reported to the high priests what had taken place (Mt 28:11). Such startling news called for an emergency session of priests and elders, and it was decided that the soldiers should be persuaded (it took quite a lot of money) to say that his disciples came by night and stole him away while they were asleep (v. 13). An obvious retort to this would surely have been, How do you know they did, if you were sleeping? Sleeping witnesses! The whole incident is so bizarre that some have questioned it. But desperate men take desperate chances. The empty tomb had to be explained. The soldiers were in a very delicate position, and for them to confess that they had been remiss in their duty was something that would have serious consequences. But they were reassured that their commander, the procurator, would be taken care of. Not to worry! He could be appeased, especially if those who had insisted upon the posting of a guard in the first place were willing to let the matter drop.

The official version of the empty tomb was, then, spread abroad and widely believed. Matthew's source for this affair was probably one of the elders, or one of the soldiers who had come to accept Christ.

The official version was a lie, of course. The apostles immediately learned the truth from Jesus himself.

CHAPTER TWELVE

The Appearances

Jesus' appearances are not interconnected; one does not lead logically to the next. One can reasonably argue that the first appearance was in Galilee. After the appearances in Jerusalem, would the apostles have returned to their fishing? Jesus may not have said much at some of his appearances, perhaps a general commission to preach the gospel which was differently formulated in various gospel traditions. In proclaiming the kingdom of heaven, the apostles came to see that their commission involved many things: baptism, the forgiveness of sins, union in a community. By the time the gospels were written, it had become clear that all this the Lord did indeed expect of them.

What emerges unmistakeably from the gospel accounts is that the risen Jesus is somehow different than he was before. Paul speaks of Jesus' body as *pneumatikos* (spiritual), not *psychikos* (variously translated as physical, natural, and animal). The risen Lord's risen body was beyond space and time. He enjoyed a different status—the women and disciples even speak of him as *Lord*. He was the same, yet not the same. In his resurrection there was continuity not only of personal existence, but of a corporeal aspect of that existence.

Emmaus

The first appearance may well have been the one to two disciples on the road to Emmaus. This charming story is one of

151

Luke's masterpieces. It is simply told. Afflicted in spirit, two disciples had set out from Jerusalem on the first day of the week, and met a stranger while on their way. They poured out their hearts to him and eventually recognized him as their Risen Lord.

The morning after Passover, two of the disciples had set out early for Emmaus, a village some sixty stadia—about seven miles—from Jerusalem (another text makes it 160 stadia). Identification of their destination is not easy. Amwas, a small town known from Maccabean times and later called Nicopolis, is about twenty miles west northwest of Jerusalem, or sixteen miles using short cuts. Another village in the same direction, El Kubebe, is only seven miles away, and here the Franciscans have built a charming little church. The site was not singled out for anything until Crusader times (1099–1187). The third possible "Emmaus" is Kolonieh. Only four miles from Jerusalem, it had once served as a military colony for 800 Roman soldiers. Josephus mentions it only as "a place," and there is little likelihood of its being the original Emmaus. Of the three possibilities, Amwas-Nicopolis stands the best chance of being correct, although that would mean two disciples covered close to forty miles in a single day—not impossible, but difficult. Possibly they returned to Jerusalem on horseback, not on foot.

The two disciples had started out early for Emmaus "that very day," on the first Easter Sunday. They were busy discussing the events of the past few days, especially the news about the empty tomb and the angels the women had seen. Jesus overtook them as they journeyed, but, like Magdalene and the apostles, they failed to recognize him. Gregory the Great thought it must have been their own fault, but it may simply have been that the risen Christ looked different, or that he did not *will* to disclose his identity just yet.

Jesus asked the travellers what they were talking about. Given this opportunity to unburden themselves, they halted, possibly to decide whether they should speak to a stranger on so sensitive a topic. In the end they decided to speak, and Cleopas asked, with dignified reserve, how anyone coming from Jerusalem could be ignorant of what everybody there was talking about. "What things?" Jesus asked, and his question was put in so sympathetic a tone and with so obvious an interest that the whole story came tumbling from Cleopas' lips. The disciples had been thinking of their leader as a prophet, even as the Messiah who, powerful in word and deed, would liberate Israel from Roman tyranny and oppression. But the unthinkable had happened: "our chief priests and rulers delivered him up . . . and crucified him." "We were hoping," he went on, "that he was the one to redeem Israel." But that was three days ago, and God had done nothing for this Jesus, or for them. To be sure, there were rumors that the women had found Jesus' tomb empty and seen some angels; the men were skeptical: if Jesus were alive he would surely have manifested himself to the disciples! None of them had seen him.

With the opening words of the stranger's reply, "O foolish men, and slow of heart," a new light begins to shine upon the cross. Behind the disciples' sadness and disappointment was their failure to appreciate all that the prophets had announced. "Did not the Messiah have to undergo all this, so as to enter into his glory?" Jesus then began, "with Moses and all the prophets," to show that the story of the Messiah had a somber side, namely, that the Messiah had to suffer. The passion was not simply a possibility but a necessity. But there was more—the Messiah was to enter into his glory. Luke does not identify the passages of the Old Testament Jesus explained, but the whole of the Old Testament revealed a divine plan so consistent that such an ending was inevitable: God's hatred for sin, and his great love for man, combined to bring about Jesus' death. The Emmaus-bound travellers had not understood the Old Testament, and so had completely misunderstood "all that had happened in Jerusalem."

The journey was coming to an end and the two disciples turned off the main road. Jesus waited to be asked to join them. With some insistence and possibly some exaggeration, they urged him to "Stay with us. It is nearly evening." He went with them. After a trip it is not unusual to sit down and eat. Courteously, they sat the stranger at the head of the table;

it was therefore toward evening. He took the bread, blessed it, then broke the bread and began to distribute it to them. And at that moment, "their eyes were opened," and they recognized their companion.

It is not likely that this meal was a eucharistic repast. After the opening action, everything stops; no mention is made of wine, and the two disciples were not among those who had been at the Last Supper. A short while later, Jesus would eat ordinary food with the apostles (24:43). Luke does not say how the disciples at Emmaus recognized Jesus, whether they saw his wounded hands, or whether he had a special way of breaking the bread. No matter. As understanding came upon them, Jesus vanished from their sight. He could will his glorified body to be visible or invisible; it was no longer subject to the ordinary physical laws of time or space. His disappearance did not sadden the disciples; rather, they realized how their hearts had been burning within them as he spoke to them about the scriptures. Their one thought now was to share their news with the Eleven. They hastened back to Jerusalem, oblivious of fatigue, and were greeted with the exciting news that Jesus had appeared to Simon. There was perhaps a note of anti-climax, then, as Cleopas and his companion related what had happened to them, and how they had come to know him in the breaking of bread. But even so, the apostles, however delirious with joy they may have been, were also no doubt wondering what it was all about.

Upon this note, the story of Emmaus ends. It showed another side of Christ—he will walk with anyone, and enkindle their hearts as they read his scriptures. Easter holds everything together, and is for all believers.

Appearance to the Disciples (Jn 20:19–21; Lk 24:36–49)

As rumors concerning the empty tomb and the missing body raced through Jerusalem, public interest ran so high that the Sanhedrin was stirred to action. The priests launched the counter rumor of grave robbery. Fearing reprisals, the disciples, Thomas excepted, drew together behind closed doors.

John mentions this significant detail to bring out the extraordinary manner of Jesus' next appearance. A hostile world may be kept at bay by doors barred and bolted, but not Jesus. He stood suddenly in the midst of his friends, and his first word was not one of recrimination, but of peace.

At the Last Supper, Jesus had spoken of peace as something he wished his followers to enjoy. It must have been reassuring to them to hear that same word on his lips now. It was more than a greeting, it was a gift. Aaron has blessed the people after offering sacrifice (Lv 9:22). After his sacrifice, Jesus who is our peace (Eph 2:14, 17) brought the blessings of peace to his disciples.

The disciples thought they were seeing things, and were understandably disturbed, for this "ghost" resembled their beloved Master. Jesus again spoke, and reassured them. "Why are you troubled, and why do questionings rise in your hearts?" he asked. Indeed, confused and ill-defined thoughts arising from unknown depths assailed their reason. Jesus then invited the apostles to put his reality to the test. Touch is something men trust. Let them touch him, then, "for a spirit does not have flesh and bones, as you see that I have. And when he had said this, he showed them his hands and his feet."

John in the parallel passage (20:20) writes: "He showed them his hands and his side." Luke and John make it clear that Jesus had been nailed to the cross and not simply bound to it.

In his glorified state the risen Christ deliberately retained the identifying marks of the passion. Old soldiers look upon their scars as proofs of past valor and loyalty; the martyrs will doubtless bear their wounds in heaven as badges of an immense honor. In Jesus' wounds the heavenly Father and the devout faithful are constantly reminded of the price the beloved Son paid for man's redemption.

Things most ardently hoped for are sometimes, when they materialize, simply too good to be true. Could this really be the Master? Jesus moved to dispel their skepticism, asking, "Have you anything here to eat?" An astonishing question, with an astonishing sequel. "They gave him a piece of broiled fish and he took it and ate before them." By partaking of this humble fare, Jesus convinced them that his body was not a spirit-body, but real; the resurrection was a fact. Salted fish was not rare in Jerusalem, and quite often formed part of the menu there.

" 'Peace be with you,' he said again. 'As the Father has sent me, so I send you' " (Jn 21:21). Peace is a disposition most favorable to God's actions. Men torn by conflict within or without can only with difficulty hear the word of God. To the now peaceful disciples, Jesus gives a commission: they shall be his apostles, sent into the world as he had been sent, invested with authority from on high, and they would be witnesses to his resurrection, proclaiming the "good news" to all the world. Jesus then breathed on them and said,

"Receive the Holy Spirit.
If you forgive the sins of any
    they are forgiven;
if you retain the sins of any,
    they are retained." (20:22–23)

The similarity of Jesus' actions and those of God are inescapable. God breathed upon Adam and made of him a living spirit; Jesus breathed on his disciples and communicated to them the Holy Spirit. This spirit, of its nature invisible, is a gift from a Jesus now glorified by the Father. At a later date, the Holy Spirit would come upon the apostles in an official, public manner on Pentecost; here Jesus gives his disciples the Spirit as a power that will ready them for the contest with sin.

Jesus foresaw that not all would keep his commandments, and he provided a merciful means for the restoration of sinners to friendship with God. The apostles would be God's instruments in the forgiving of sins. Naturally, they would not use this power indiscriminately, for it was a judicial power, and the disposition of the sinner has also to be considered. The sacrament of penance has then a firm biblical foundation.

What the scripture does not say is often very significant. The text does not say that Jesus departed from them. . . The gift of the Spirit involves the abiding presence of Jesus in the midst of his own.

The Doubting Thomas (John 20:24–29)

A composite picture of Thomas the apostle shows him to be energetic, generous, material-minded, impressionable, and stubborn. Loyal to a fault, he was also somewhat skeptical. When the women informed him that they had seen the risen Lord, he refused to believe them. Nor did he believe the news when he heard it from his fellow apostles. Their statement, "We have seen the Lord," fell on deaf ears. Of a positivist disposition, he made it clear that he would not believe unless he could verify the fact for himself. Possibly there was something of the rugged individualist in Thomas. It is not impossible that he felt a twinge of disappointment, perhaps even resentment, that Jesus had shown himself when he, Thomas, was absent. It is instructive, in a way, that Jesus was in no hurry to smooth Thomas' ruffled feathers. While the others rejoiced, Thomas held himself aloof.

"Eight days later, his disciples were again in the house, and Thomas was with them" (20:26). The doors were again shut, but Jesus suddenly appeared in the midst of his friends. "Peace be with you" was on his lips. Then, using Thomas' own words (how did he come to know them?) he reproved that apostle for his stubbornness. "Put your finger here and see my hands, and put out your hand and place it in my side. Do not be faithless but believing."

The gospels do not say whether Thomas persisted in his skepticism and actually verified the fact of Jesus' wounds. What he did do was to make the first explicit act of faith in the divinity of the Risen Christ, saying: "[You are] my Lord and my God."

As Dodd has noted, the Thomas episode takes place on the boundary of the empirical and the spiritual world. The apostle's words are more than an exclamation of wonder or thanksgiving: they are an expression of faith, and might be paraphrased by: "Yes, it is Jesus, and he is divine." Here, in this climactic moment, the Old Testament's words for God and the Lord are applied to Jesus. The Word made flesh is finally recognized as the Word that was God.

Credulity is not a virtue. Thomas was not at fault because he demanded proof, but on the other hand, he was not to be commended for insisting that he see with his own eyes. There is a *fides oculata*, a faith that sees. Jesus said to Thomas, "Blessed are those who have not seen and yet believe." This saying has been dubbed "the ninth beatitude," and it represents the true climax of the gospel. Jesus is now in another world, and it is through faith that future generations of believers see him. Every believing reader of the gospel can learn from Jesus' words to Thomas. Christian faith depends upon the conviction that "Jesus is the Christ, the Son of God, and . . . believing, you may have life in his name."

The Last Appearance (Mt 28:1–16; Jn 21:1–25)

The scene has abruptly and surprisingly changed. The apostles are back in Galilee, as instructed (Mt 28:7). They had gathered somewhere along the shore of the Sea of Galilee, once so familiar to them. They numbered seven, five of whom are named: Simon Peter, Thomas (also called Didymus, or the Twin), Nathanael (also known as Bartholomew?) of Cana in Galilee, the sons of Zebedee (they are found only in the Fourth Gospel), and two others. It is odd to find Thomas and Nathanael in the group; their professions are unknown. Perhaps they were instinctively drawn to Peter.

After all that had happened, it is surprising that the apostles returned to their old way of life, but as yet they knew no other. Jesus had on two occasions (Jn 17:18; 20:21) spoken of them as being "sent," but the word lacked precision. Sent where? Why? His words represented their investiture or commission; their actual mission to the Gentiles was launched very soon (at Pentecost). As yet, Jesus had not formally ascended to his Father, so they did not yet have to assume their roles as his spokesmen. While in Galilee, therefore, they did the only thing they knew they were good at—they went fishing.

Once again it is Peter who took the initiative: "I am going fishing" (Jn 21:3). Indeed, it is still customary to fish at night in the Sea of Galilee. This time, unaccountably, they had no luck; they caught nothing. As day began to break, John writes, the apostles saw Jesus standing on the shore. The disciples had seen him twice already, but they did not recognize him. It may have been that the visibility was poor, or that for some reason, Jesus did not wish to be recognized.

Jesus hailed the men in the boat, in almost predictable words: "You fellows, you haven't got a bit of fish, have you?" (*Paidia, me ti prosphagion echete?*) (v. 5), sounding like a man looking for something to eat for breakfast. They answered with a short unqualified "no," which spoke volumes: fishermen hate to confess that they have caught no fish. At the moment they may have been set to make another try, and just then Jesus called out, "Cast the net on the right side of the boat, and you will find some" (v. 6). Could he have seen a school of fish they could not see? Was there a note of command in his words that got though to them? There is no question but that they had tried the right side of the boat before, perhaps many times during the night. One more time? Fishermen are the most hopeful of men. They followed his suggestion, and their net was filled with so many fish that they could not haul in the net.

Peter and John, in the story we have, run true to form. John had a keener intuition, and Peter was a quick reactor. In the midst of this great wriggling haul of fish, that disciple whom Jesus loved said to Peter, "It is the Lord" (v. 7). At this point the great ascetic, St. Jerome, ranged in true patristic style far beyond the text, saying: "Virginity recognized the virginal body [of Christ] first." He was not necessarily wrong in this, either. Many times in the life of the Church, there arise privileged souls who recognize Jesus before the captain at the helm does. Jesus sometimes entrusts to them secrets which they are to draw to Peter's attention. Catherine of Siena, such a privileged one, brought the message to an anxious Pope. At John's words, Peter reacted, as was his custom. "He put on his clothes and sprang into the sea." The term for the garment he put on is *ependutes*, an outer garment or smock one put on over his clothes; it probably resembled a laboratory coat or a large apron, a smock. Peter must have tightened his sash so that the garment would not impede his swimming, and plunged into the water.

While Peter was swimming to shore, the other disciples brought the boat in, some of them manning oars, others holding on to the bulging net. John estimated that the boat was about a hundred yards offshore. When the boat was finally landed, they saw a fire, a heap of glowing embers. This scene is recorded by John alone, but Peter would undoubtedly remember another fire . . .

"Bring some of the fish that you have just caught," the stranger ordered (v. 10). They were to offer something at their disposal, then, but it would not be needed, nor used. They brought him some of the fish, Simon Peter helping drag the net onto the shore.

John records the number of fish exactly: There were 153 fish in the net. This has triggered a spate of fanciful, intriguing interpretations on the part of the ancients about the meaning of the number. Some have said that the 153 fish represent one of each species of fish, a perfect catch (Ez 47:10; Mt 13:47). In fact, alas, there are only twenty-two species of fish in the Sea of Galilee. To Jerome the variety of fish indicated that there was to be no racial or any kind of bar in the Church. Origen, ever on the lookout for hidden meanings, found it in the 3: 153 consists of three 50s plus one 3; obviously, a symbol of the Trinity! Cyril of Alexandria saw in the number the future proportions of the church: 100 pagans, 50 Jews, presided over by the Trinity. Augustine, noting that 153 is the sum of the consecutive numbers 1+2 . . . 17, noted that 17 is made up of the numbers 10 and 7, which stand for the Ten Commandments and the Seven Gifts of the Holy Spirit. Modern fans of numbers have discovered that one can arrive at 153 by adding up the numerical value of the letters that spell out the Hebrew *qahal hahavah*, which means "the Church of Love." It is not clear that these speculations mean anything, but they always exercise a certain fascination for some.

After the apostles counted the fish, they found that Jesus already had fish broiling on some coals, and some bread. Where had these victuals come from? We do not know. However, it is obvious that Jesus was always the teacher. The apostles would obtain great results if they followed his directions. They were also to remember that he does not depend upon them for food; it was the other way around. But he would use something that they could bring.

Peter went aboard and hauled the net ashore, full of the fish. His presence there was natural enough. As captain he was the one who lifted the net out of the water, or directed others in such a fashion that the net would not be torn or damaged. That the fish should have been counted is not unusual; the number had to be known so that the catch could be divided in an equitable manner between captain and crew.

That the net contained so large a number of big fish (John notes that they were "big" fish) gives the net which did not break under the strain a special significance. The earliest commentators were not slow to see in it a symbol of the Church which remains one however many peoples it contains.

" 'Come and have breakfast,' Jesus said to them. None of the disciples was bold enough to ask, 'Who are you?' They knew [quite well] it was the Lord" (v. 12). In fact, Jesus had not identified himself, nor greeted them with the customary "Peace," nor did he exhibit his wounded hands and feet to them. But he was not bound always to manifest himself in familiar ways. Following his direction, the apostles had done their work. Now he serves them with the bread and fish he had prepared for them. He is the host; they are his guests. He was teaching them that without his help, their efforts would fail.

Throughout this whole scene, it is not so much the words as the facts and the actions which are important; these indeed speak volumes.

Jesus then "stepped forward, took the bread and gave it to them, and so with the fish. This was now the third time that Jesus was revealed to the disciples after he was raised from the dead" (21:14).

The Primacy of Peter

BEGIN

After eating a strange meal with a mysterious stranger on a once familiar shore, the disciples fell silent. The free and easy camaraderie with the Master no longer prevailed. Jesus then said to Simon, " 'Simon, son of John, do you love me more than these others?' Peter answered, 'Yes, Lord; you know that I love you' " (Jn 21:15).

Earlier, Jesus had promised Peter the primacy; he was different from the others (see Mt 16:13–20). Peter was the first to voice his belief that Jesus was the Messiah and Son of God, and at that time Jesus had called him a rock, saying, "upon this rock I will build my church." The "rock" had its rough edges, for Peter would deny his Master three times. But Peter's denials would be offset by a threefold affirmation of love amid circumstances that gave a special solemnity to this moment: an unusual catch of fish, a stranger who turned out to be the Lord, the early morning hour by the fire, all this contributed to a sense of awe and mystery. Simon Peter was singled out for special attention and given a singular position and task. His answers to Jesus' questions were of prime importance; it was essential that he answer correctly, and he did. After the thrice-repeated question, he appealed to Jesus' special knowledge, saying with humility: "Lord, you know everything. You *know* that I love you" (v. 17). Peter would never again boast, as he once had, about the superior quality of *his* love (Mt. 26:33).

In the Greek text two different words are used for "love" and two different words for "feed." The variety may be explained simply; John avoided the monotony of repetition. There are no significant nuances of meaning in the words. It is however highly significant that Peter alone was singled out to receive from the Good Shepherd, the power to serve and govern his lambs and his sheep. The shepherd was being invested into his office of caring for the faithful.

The shepherd image is a familiar one. The guardians of the sheep were not all equally good; sheep often suffered at the hands of bad ones. The Lord had assured his people that he would raise up shepherds to feed the sheep. The flock might dwindle to a remnant, but shepherds would be provided. In speaking to Peter as he did, Jesus was giving him a genuine power over his sheep. Himself the Good Shepherd (John 10), he would set a good example by dying for his sheep, and Peter would in the end die for his, thus giving glory to God. His death would show how closely he was united to his Master, and that he was a perfect disciple, a good shepherd, and good, solid rock.

The apostles under Peter's leadership, were to take care of all believers in Jesus Christ. The shepherd image is a better one than that of the fisherman to describe this commission; fish die when taken out of their element, whereas those who are "caught" for (and by) the Savior go on living. Peter is head and chief shepherd of all who tend the flock of Christ. High up in the nave of St. Peter's in Rome, the words "feed my lambs, feed my sheep" are a constant reminder to the Pope of his obligations toward his flock.

The precise meaning of the primacy of Peter has been (and is still) disputed. Was Peter (and are his successors) the supreme pontiff, or as the phrase goes, merely *primus inter pares*, first among equals, occupants of a primatial see? Were Peter's prerogatives given to him for a time only, or were they transmissible to those who came after him? Did they end with his death? Is his primacy to be considered a primacy in love, nothing more? And finally, can one detect in John's last chapter traces of a rivalry that once existed between Peter and the Beloved Disciple, two men of vital importance to the Christian community? Christian tradition points steadily to the authority of Peter's primacy and that of his successors.

It can certainly be said that the power of the keys was given to Peter alone. However much the other apostles shared in his work of evangelization, the text does not "give" them the keys. The supreme authority was for Peter alone. The apostles are foundation stones, but they rest upon the rock that is Peter.

Peter's Destiny

Jesus now predicts an added glory for Peter, namely, that he will one day imitate the Good Shepherd in his death.

I tell you solemnly;
as a young man
you fastened your belt
and went about as you pleased;
but when you are older
you will stretch out your hands,
and another will tie you fast
and carry you off against your will.

The solemn "Amen, amen" used here is exclusively Johannine. Peter was at the time in the prime of his life, between youth and old age (he swam ashore to meet his Lord). "To fasten one's belt" means to be in control of one's actions, to be able to take care of oneself. A young man goes wherever he wants to go; not so the old. "To stretch out one's hands" is a gesture of dependence, characteristic of the very young and the old. Others straighten the clothing of the old and the young, and old people bow to the will of those who are younger, go where *they* choose. Since the text says nothing about the kind of death Peter was to die, the meaning of Jesus' words became clear only after Peter had been crucified; the evangelist notes this carefully. According to the apocryphal writings, Peter was crucified upside-down on Vatican Hill, tied to the cross with ropes. "Against your will" probably refers not to Peter's unwillingness to suffer for his Master, but to the natural revulsion to such a death.

"When Jesus had finished speaking he said to him, 'Follow me.' " Peter would soon learn that love does not make life easy, that his duties would in fact become more exacting, and his personal freedom more restricted as time went on. But what of the Beloved Disciple? Once at the Last Supper that disciple had asked a question for Peter (13:25) and Peter will now return the favor. What would "following Jesus" mean in John's case? The question is quite natural and need not have been prompted by curiosity or jealousy. Peter understands he is to die; will John also have to die? "What about him?"

From other sources we know that John's great contribution

would be that of a man of thought rather than of action, as a writer of the profound, mystical appreciation of Christ which we know as the Fourth Gospel. His would be a different vocation from that of Peter. That is all Peter has to know. All he has to do is what the Lord wills—to *feed* the flock, and leave the fate of the sheep in the Lord's hands.

Jesus' words about John—"Suppose I want him to stay until I come?"—might be interpreted to mean that John was to live until the end of time, but John corrects this view. He had not said "that the disciple was not going to die: all he said was, 'Suppose I want him to stay until I come?' " That was not Peter's concern. The words however formed a basis for a tradition that John lived to a ripe old age. Little is known of John's later years, but one tradition has it that he died at Ephesus.

Apostolic Mission (Mt 28:16–20)

Matthew's interest in the Church, a theme which underlies his gospel, is especially evident in his account of Jesus' appearance to the disciples in Galilee. It is the only appearance Matthew records, and it is characteristic that his *mise en scène* is an unspecified mountain in Galilee. Nothing better illustrates the freedom with which the evangelists handled their material. Luke centered everything in Jerusalem. There the apostles began their preaching (24:47; Acts 1:8), there the angel appeared to Zechariah in the Temple to announce the birth of the Precursor, and there the Promised One had died. Matthew's gospel ends in Galilee, where the angel had appeared to Mary, seeking her consent to become the mother of Jesus, where that Son had first preached the Good News, and where he had chosen the Twelve.

At the sight of the Risen Lord, "those who had doubted fell down in homage before him." This interesting remark suggests that Matthew knew that Jesus' appearances elsewhere had provoked doubt, a doubt that had to be settled before the apostles would be given their mission. It is not said how the doubt was dispelled, but it is clear that the apostles belief in the resurrection was not due to an unquestioning religious enthusiasm, but rather to the overpowering experience of seeing and speaking with their crucified Master who was alive.

" 'All authority' he said, 'in heaven and on earth has been given to me.' " The resurrection may have separated Christ from his disciples, but it gave him a power which he had hitherto enjoyed only in a limited way. He is now the exalted Son of Man who has already been to heaven and is in full possession of the state of glory. The *therefore* has a special significance: he has the right to outline for them the course of action:

"Go therefore and make disciples
of all the nations."

Mark in his independent version of this command says much the same thing:

"Go into all the world, and
proclaim the Good News to all creatures."

The scope of both commands is universal, and marks a development in the plan of salvation. Jesus had deliberately restricted his ministry to the flock of Israel, chosen by God to be the light of the nations, and the vehicle through which the saving plan should be brought to all men. But Israel had rejected the role, not only in Palestine but throughout the Diaspora, as Acts makes clear. The divine plan was then modified, and the faithful few who had welcomed the Christ were to bring the message directly to the pagan nations. Thus was the ancient prophecy fulfilled. The mission of the apostles was as universal as the power behind it. Here in a nutshell is the heart of Christianity, a genuine saying of Jesus himself, and one independently reported by Matthew and by Mark:

"Baptizing them in the name
of the Father, and of the Son,
and of the Holy Spirit."

Baptism is a washing with water. As a sacrament it is a sign that the person washed is being initiated into a believing community. No other precept has been so faithfully and so universally practiced, for it rests upon the very words of Christ. Baptism is as old as Christianity, but it has evolved in a dynamic way—from immersion in the waters of a stream or a baptismal font, to the pouring of water upon the head. It is not surprising that the practical difficulties of baptism by immersion should have developed in such a way that the substance of the symbolic action be preserved in a simpler kind of washing. Changes in non-essentials are well within the Church's competence, and she has not hesitated to exercise that right for the good of the faithful.

The baptismal formula in Matthew is expressed in trinitarian terms which are specifically and uniquely Christian. In the Acts, however, people are said to have been baptized "in the name of Jesus," and Christians were known as "those who invoked the name of the Lord," that is, of Jesus. It is of course possible that in apostolic times, which were under the prompting of the Holy Spirit, people were baptized in the name of Jesus. Or the words may simply have described in juridic fashion a baptism which was administered on Jesus' authority, distinct therefore from other baptismal rites familiar to the Jews. Matthew's trinitarian formula may in truth reflect the liturgical usage established in the course of time by the primitive Christian community.

"Teaching them to observe all that
I have commanded you."

The new life which is offered to mankind will not be simple. It is not enough to be baptized and to repent; the believer must observe Christ's commands. He must lead the new life day by day, often at the cost of sacrifice. And there is always more to be learned. Instruction precedes but does not halt there with baptism. The duty of teaching devolves upon the hierarchy. Prophets, appearing at unpredictable intervals, had been teachers of Israel; the Scribes were likewise teachers in Israel, but what they offered was not adequate. Now the apostles shall preach in season and out of season, and their message shall be: Do whatever he tells you.

"And lo, I am with you always,
until the end of the world."

Jesus' last words are more than a farewell; they are a promise. He will be spiritually present in the Church as her constant source of life. Through that Church, he himself is made available to all. The gates of hell will not prevail against the Church, for the powers of evil and of darkness are less powerful than he. With the Father and the Holy Spirit, Jesus is with his missionaries, and it is the divine power that shall cause their work to succeed throughout future ages. Consoling words. What will take place after the end is beyond imagining. Enough for his disciples to carry out his command to make all men his disciples.⌉ EN⫸

CHAPTER THIRTEEN

The Ascension

The resurrection narratives come to an end with Jesus' ascension into heaven, recorded once by Mark (16:19–20) and twice by Luke (24:50–53 and Acts 1:9–12). In his gospel, Luke notes that the disciples afterwards returned to Jerusalem with great joy, praising and blessing God in the temple; in Acts, they returned to the Upper Room, praying with Jesus' mother and several other women.

The ascension took place somewhere between Jerusalem and Bethany, and by 375 A.D. an octagonal building was built near the top of the Mount of Olives to commemorate the event.

The gospel story is simply told and is free of embellishment. Jesus led the disciples out as far as Bethany, and while blessing them, was carried up into heaven (Lk 24:51). A cloud hid him from their sight (Acts 1:9), and he took his seat at the right hand of God (Mk 16:19).

Jesus' ascension, like the resurrection, has come under heavy attack. Believers, however, balk at a methodology which excludes *a priori* the possibility of divine acts in history. For some (not for us), a thorough-going naturalistic approach to history is the only "scientific" or "objective" approach. The man of faith is much more open-minded. To him, the "scientific" method is misleading and impossibly rigid.

One can candidly concede that there are difficulties attached to the account of Jesus' ascension. A balance has to be maintained between history and a written record which involves biblical imagery. The ascension may not be historically verifiable in a strict sense, but it is not mythological nonsense. What we must deal with in the accounts of the ascension is biblical "picture-language," a special mode of writing all can understand. For example, there is an Old Testament flavor to the words "he [Jesus] was taken up." One recalls that Elijah (2 Kgs 2:1) and Enoch (Sir 44:16) were both "taken up." It is easy for critics to scoff at this image if they take it literally. A recent example of this was the statement of an atheistic Russian astronaut who announced that he had nowhere seen God in space.

Spatial metaphors are very common. How natural it is to associate God with height! We constantly speak in such terms: men receive a high salary, or high marks; there is always room at the top. Many good things come from "up there": warmth and light from the sun, the air, and the rain that causes things to grow. What the evangelists intended when they wrote that Jesus had been "taken up," was not something verifiable in physical terms, but rather that Jesus' visible presence on earth had come to an end, and that he was going to his Father, where he now lives in a world where time and space are without meaning.

Jesus is now seated at the right hand of God, Mark says. The symbol has to be handled carefully. God has no body, nor does he live in a heavenly mansion filled with gilded thrones. In saying that Jesus now sits at God's right hand, Mark really was saying that Jesus is highly exalted, equal to God himself, for an inferior does not sit in the presence of the king. In many cultures, the "right" side is more honorable than the left (with apologies to the 13 percent of us who are left-handed!). A favored person is a Benjamin, i.e., a "son of the right hand." It is an interesting fact that this view has become a part of protocol: in processions, or even in so ordinary a matter as a stroll, the VIP or important person is, in Europe at least, kept on one's right.

There is also the fact that Jesus is now invested with heavenly power and dignity, *in his risen human nature.* The Incarnation then was not a fleeting, but a divine action with permanent consequences: Jesus' human nature is now wherever Jesus is. We can say then, that a man *like us* now sits in God's presence. What an antidote to depression, or to a feeling of worthlessness. Our human nature has been and is forever honored. Sinful man can lift his head on high, and what is more, he can hope.

Luke says in Acts (but not in his gospel) that Jesus showed himself alive to his disciples, appearing to them during forty days (Act 1:3). One is intrigued by these forty days. What filled them? Where were they spent? Did Jesus appear suddenly, startling his followers? That he instructed his apostles seems clear enough, but for so long a period? Was his final victory over sin and death, and his exaltation, deferred for forty days, and if so, why?

It seems much more natural to suppose that Jesus entered into his Father's presence to receive his reward at the very moment of his resurrection. His reply to the good thief was: "Today you will be with me in paradise" (Lk 23:43), and he admonished Mary Magdalene (Jn 20:17) not to hold onto him for he was "ascending to his Father."

The number forty is used so often in the Bible that it calls for a careful look. History does not happen in regular patterns of forty days or years (What does our own expression, to take "forty winks" tell us?). One can, however, hold for an immediate ascension of Jesus into heaven, and for a definitive departure some time later.

A cloud eventually hid Jesus from the apostles' sight. There is no question here of cirrus or cumulus clouds; it is rather a biblical reference. In the Old Testament and in the gospel accounts of Jesus' transfiguration, a cloud was often the symbol of God's presence. For Jesus to enter the cloud meant that he was now in God's presence. The apostles were then given instructions what they were to do. They were to get on with living. Jesus may have disappeared, but he would come again (1 Thes 4:17; Rv 11:12), and until then, they were to go out and preach the gospel until Jesus, now reigning in glory, comes again.

Epilogue

For two thousand years now, Jesus of Nazareth has been the cause of divergent opinions. His relatives thought he was out of his mind (Mk 3:20). His fellow Jews looked on him as a stumbling-block, a scandal. Greeks wrote him off as a foolish fellow (1 Cor 1:23). Yet he was also admired, loved, and adored by many. He is the reason why Christianity is a world religion. Although he scarcely ever went beyond the confines of his own land, his teachings have influenced the thinking and the lives of millions. This is all the more remarkable because from a human point of view he was a public failure and died a disgraceful death.

Jesus has never been easy to understand. He transcends the categories into which famous people fit. His story, what there is of it, is found in the New Testament, and makes fascinating reading, for there men and women of every age learn of the breathtaking possibilities of everlasting life in the kingdom of God. After reading his story and hearing his words, one cannot simply close the book on Jesus and forget him. One chooses.

For a number of reasons, some prefer not to follow Jesus Christ and his teachings. Let us take a look at some of their reasons.

The Hard Way

Jesus, a peerless orator and a healer of the sick, was constantly in the public eye. Popular acclaim meant little to him, however, and he often went off by himself to pray. He made it clear that he expected his followers to be prepared for drastic action. They would in fact have to be ready to die for him. "Whoever would save his life will lose it, and whoever loses his life for my sake will find it" (Mt 16:24). He himself was marked for death—it was impossible that he did not see this— yet he marched resolutely toward Jerusalem where death awaited him. He was consistent. From the first he urged his listeners to rely upon their heavenly Father who had a care for the birds of the air and the lilies of the field. He often chided his timorous disciples, saying: "Why were you frightened?" or "Fear not." He set them an example by his own trust and courage.

Men do not willingly assume difficult tasks unless these involve the possibility of success and great rewards. When a leader inspires confidence, all difficulties can be faced. During the last World War, for example, Churchill told his beleagured countrymen: "I have nothing to offer you but blood, toil, tears, and sweat." Magnificent words, these; they became a sort of rallying cry, offsetting fear and despair and sparking a great effort against a human enemy that led ultimately to victory.

Jesus was engaged in a much more fearful struggle, against the father of lies, the devil, and the enemy within every man, the sinful self. The victory sought in his case was a victory over sin and death; the prize to be won was freedom, truth, and life.

A strange thing about Jesus is his impact, not just upon humanity, but upon every individual. He is every man's savior, his words are addressed to all. If today his followers are numbered by the millions, it is because they have recognized his words of eternal life, and because he has himself first trodden the hard way to victory. The gate may be narrow, and the way hard (Mt 7:14), but the struggle becomes a high adventure calling for great personal effort. There is consistency here also. When Jesus worked his miracles, he gave his followers something to do also: the apostles had to haul in the net filled with fish and, on another occasion, distributed the loaves and fishes he had miltiplied. Others were sent to wash in the pool of Siloam, or to tell the priests what had happened, or to give a little ten-year old girl something to eat! Jesus was not a one-man show. His followers were active participants in his saving work.

In writing about the Incarnation, Thomas Aquinas notes how delicately God made room for man's participation in the divine plan of salvation. The plan was more than a divine edict; it was the undoing of man's sin, a work of restoration in which human beings were personally involved. God seems to have gone out of his way to restore self-esteem in fallen man. The very human Virgin Mary was courteously interviewed and God's wishes were explained to her, but nothing happened until she had assented to whatever it was God willed. Like every other human, Mary's child was born a tiny baby, grew up in a family, and, when grown up, served his heavenly Father in time and space. At the end of his life he displayed to heaven and earth a magnificent act of love—his redemptive death. Now indeed man has good reason to lift up his head. God's Son became incarnate in our humanity, and in it suffered and died for all men. Jesus assured his listeners that the very hairs of their heads were numbered, and that they were worth more than the sparrows over which the Father watched (Mt 10:30–31); his death was a magnificent proof of those words.

It is not easy to follow in the footsteps of this Master. Teresa of Avila, a great mystic who was habitually aware of God's presence in the depths of her heart, wrote of a time when he seemed to absent himself from her for several days. When he again made his presence known, she asked him tartly where he had been, and why she had been deprived of his presence for so long. He replied mildly that he treated all his friends like that. "Small wonder you have so few, then," said she. The road to God is by a hard road and a narrow gate, and many turn from it.

The Mysterious Way

A modern author, Rudolf Otto, speaks of God as the *mysterium tremendum et fascinans*, as the tremendous, fascinating mystery. He is God and we are creatures. Not all like mystery. Most people prefer to be "in the know," but God is always mysterious. We learn something of what God is like because he has chosen to reveal something of himself. Because he is intelligent and has a plan, we know that he is a personal God, not an ill-defined "force." We also know that he is a "moral" God: he has made all things good, and is intolerant of evil. He is also loving, for he generously shares his life and his grace with man whose future is to dwell with him.

As we discover from reading the Bible, God graciously took an active interest in the destiny of the human race. He established a covenant between himself and his Chosen People; they were to be his faithful people and he would be their God. This part of God's plan did not fully succeed, for his people proved to be unfaithful. After wandering the desert for forty years, they entered into the Promised Land, but their stay there was brief, and soon—a few hundred years later—they were carried off into exile.

God renewed his covenants with Noah, Abraham, Moses, and others, and intimated to Jeremiah that there would one day be a new and everlasting covenant. This was realized amid poverty and hardship; the blood that sealed the new covenant was that of Jesus, proclaimed by a voice from a cloud as "My well-beloved Son!"

Mysterious are the ways of God. We are his creatures, he is the creator. We cannot presume to deal with him on equal terms, but only with deference and respect. As God proclaimed through Isaiah: "As the heavens are higher than the earth, so are my ways higher than your ways, and my thoughts than your thoughts" (55:8). The day will come when mortal man may, with God's help, see him face to face, and begin to appreciate the infinite wisdom of the God who made him, entered into a loving covenant with him, and saved him.

With the eyes of faith, one perceives the fascinating mystery of God; without it, one sees only absurdities.

The Suffering Way

Suffering is not an abstract thing, but as real as a toothache or a broken bone. No one enjoys it. Yet Christ called upon his followers to face it bravely. "If any man would come after me, let him deny himself, and take up his cross daily, and follow me" (Lk 9:23). His listeners were counselled to "Take my yoke upon you and learn from me, for I am gentle and lowly in heart. My yoke is easy, and my burden light" (Mt 11:30). It would seem that Christians, even if they are enjoying good health and success in life, are expected to suffer and to be happy about it. In truth, there is no Christianity without the cross.

The churches have sometimes been criticized for doing too little to relieve human suffering and to improve social conditions. In one sense, this criticism is most unfair, for Christians have a most honorable record in efforts to relieve the ills of mankind. But Christians also know something else: that man, by nature, is not an earthbound but a spiritual being. That is why he persists in lifting up his heart, and looking beyond the present. The Psalmist praised God for having made man little less than a god (the old translations have "than the angels"). Despite that spiritual nature, man is well acquainted with sickness and suffering, and where possible, struggles to overcome them. His inward attitude is the all-important thing. The measure of his human fulfillment is the way in which he accepts and bears his crosses, the courage he manifests in his sufferings, and the dignity he displays when facing doom and disaster. The Christian is not overly concerned with the conditions of his life because he has a "why" to live for. Life is his opportunity to follow in the footsteps of the Lord Jesus, who suffered willingly, out of love, in order to save man from sin and death.

Christians are convinced that however urgent physical and social ills may be, the ultimate cause of man's ills is sin. Sin is not a popular subject, and has been swept under many a rug. One can always find pseudo-theologians who will "take away the sins of the world" by calling all sins "socially unacceptable behavior, the result of one's genes, or of one's environment or lack of education." The saints were realistic about sin. They perceived that sin flourishes in a man's soul when he denies that he has sinned or hides his misdeeds under multi-syllabic words. Better by far to accept responsiblity for one's behavior, to acknowledge that our sins are the causes of our alienation from God, and that we desperately need to repent of them and to receive forgiveness.

From Genesis to Revelation, the Bible presents sin as an evil. In due course, Jesus was caught up in the battle between good and evil; here was spiritual combat at its fiercest. He came to save man from sin, and he did so by dying for him. If there is no such thing as sin, the crucifixion and our redemption have no meaning. For anyone who has eyes to see, sin is all about us.

It is a melancholy fact that man often abuses his freedom and commits those sins which isolate him from God and his fellow man. His sins pile up a debt that must be paid. How great a debt? Affronts are measured by the dignity of the person offended (it is less dangerous to insult a fellow worker than the head of the company), but payment for affronts is measured by the dignity of the debtor. As a crime that offends God, then, sin incurs an infinite debt. Who on earth can undo the damage? Only one who while being divine, is also one with sinful humanity. His name is Jesus Christ.

Theological symbols help bring out the meaning and value of Jesus' suffering and death. Man's restoration to God's friendship required *expiation*, that is, a "rubbing out" or "erasure" of the stain. The word *satisfaction* introduces the honest note of justice; it "does enough" to offset the damage done by sin. *Propiation* is a word that describes the desired result of satisfaction for sin, namely, that God is appeased and rendered once again friendly toward sinners. *Atonement* refers to the final result of the above activity, namely, God and man are again *at-one*.

These words, feeble candles at best, shed some light on the drama of Calvary. In the New Testament, Jesus' death was both the saving act of God and Jesus' voluntary sacrifice of himself. What Jesus offered to his Father on Calvary was not satisfaction in the sense of punishment, nor any material reparation in the shape of suffering; it was, rather, an astonishing act of humility and love and obedience.

It was this supreme act of love on Jesus' part that opened for man the gates of heaven and "captured" mankind for God. At the very moment when evil seemed triumphant, when God's saving plan appeared to have been sabotaged by the forces of evil, Jesus became for himself and for all men the master of life and of death. Gerard Manley Hopkins has given magnificent expression to this paradox in his poem, *The Windhover*. The soaring kestrel riding the wind speaks to him of Christ. The bird in its downward plunge demonstrates its mastery over the air; Christ's "fall" was his great moment of victory. A black, seemingly lifeless coal crumbles, and as it does, reveals its glowing interior, suggesting in its gold-vermillion, the gashes and wounds and suffering of Christ, and also his inward beauty and life.

There are profound resonances here to St. Paul, who wrote to the Galatians, "Far be it from me to glory except in the cross of our Lord Jesus Christ, by which the world has been crucified to me, and I to the world" (6:14).

Jesus is challenging, mysterious, acquainted with suffering, and our friend and savior. He came into the world to save sinners. "To the King of ages, the immortal, the invisible, the only God, be honor and glory forever and ever! Amen" (1 Tm 1:17).

Christians and Jews

The Jews are a remarkable people. Representing less than one percent of the world's population, they have produced an astonishing number of talented people: singers, writers, musicians, scientists, doctors, lawyers, entertainers, stage and screen stars, business geniuses. Their story, half of which is to be found in what we call the Bible, extends over four millenia. In it one encounters Abraham and the patriarchs, Moses the great liberator, colorful kings and impressive prophets, and famous women as well: Miriam and Deborah, Ruth and Naomi, Bathsheba, Athaliah and Jezebel. Saints and sinners, both. They knew all about life. At first a nomadic people, they settled in Egypt and prospered, until, under a Pharaoh "who knew not Joseph" (Ex 1:8), they were subjected to forced labor. To escape this, they followed Moses into the fearful desert, and survived, a free people. Under Joshua they entered the Promised Land. Their golden age spanned the reigns of David and Solomon, but after that it was schism and exile. Only a remnant survived the Babylonian experience, and returned to their land. Their ancestral religion clashed with the culture and charm of Greece, and then the Jews found themselves subject to the strong arm of Rome. The night was dark indeed, and there was no prophet in the land. Suddenly there appeared first a humble couple, Joseph and Mary, Jesus of Nazareth, then Peter, head of a group (mostly fishermen) called the Twelve, and an extraordinary man named Paul of Tarsus—all of them Jews the world can never forget, or thank enough.

How did the Jews manage to survive desert, war, exile, oppression? By their spiritual strength. They believed they were the Chosen People, a people of the Promise. They believed in their covenant with an unseen God under whom they were passionately committed to justice, peace, and freedom. They were keepers of the flame that Christianity was to bring to all the nations. Thus Jews and Christians together are crucial to all humanity, and to humanity's political, spiritual, and cultural survival.

Throughout history, Jews have been hated and despised, sometimes by and sometimes along with Christians. Persian pogroms and Babylonian persecutions, Roman mistrust and ridicule, have been replaced by modern ostracism and contempt. Shocking and false charges have been levelled against Jews: they were eaters of children, disturbers of the peace, and untrustworthy; that their ambition was to control the world. They flourished in Alexandria and Rome and elsewhere in the far-flung diaspora, but they were also expelled from Rome twice, once by Tiberius in 19 A.D., and again by Claudius in 49 A.D.

When Constantine became the first Christian emperor, the Jews found that Christians could be worse than pagans, for the accusation of deicide was added to the ancient canards. Jews were held by many to be collectively and corporately guilty of Christ's death; upon their brows was not the mark of Cain, but the curse of God himself. On various occasions, therefore, kings and princes "righteously" confiscated Jewish property, and imposed upon Jews cruel and humiliating restrictions. The harsh treatment of this minority group has seldom abated, and anti-Semitism has remained.

The Popes and Anti-Semitism

The picture, however, is not uniformly black. The last century has seen a series of strong, courageous popes who have spoken out in behalf of the downtrodden. Pius XI's brief statement: "Spiritually we are all Semites" (cf. Jn 4:22), openly challenged the Nazi glorification of the Aryan race. During the second World War, Pius XII provided asylum and protection for thousands of Jews. He did not publicly denounce the Nazi treatment of the Jews (and others), obviously not because he approved the Nazi excesses, but because he felt that such a statement would have produced more harm than good (a view, incidentally, that was shared by Churchill and Roosevelt). During the same period, the future John XXIII was performing many acts of charity toward the Jews in Istanbul. When he became Pope, he directed that unfavorable references to Jews and Judaism be removed from the liturgy. Nor did he stop there. He startled the world by announcing, on January 25, 1959, that he intended to convoke an Ecumenical Council wherein the Church would consider its role in the modern world. One of the items on the agenda was to be Jewish-Christian relationships. In 1960, he greeted a visiting Jewish group with the touching words, "I am Joseph (that was his baptismal name), your brother" (cf. Gn 45:3), and spoke of their mutual hopes for better relationships.

The Council began on October 11, 1962 and ended on December 8, 1965. Among the shining achievements of its four sessions was the *Declaration on Non-Christian Religions*, approved by a vote of 2312 to 88 on October 28, 1965. It is known as the *Nostra Aetate* (from its opening words). A mere six pages in length, it is, in the eyes of many far from Christ, the Church's passport to credibility. It acknowledges the religious longings and searching for God of non-Christian religions: "The Church rejects nothing that is true and holy" in Hinduism, Buddhism, Islam, and other religions. Three pages of the Declaration have to do with the "people of the covenants, of the Law, of the worship, and of the promise" (Rom 9:4f), and it is specifically stated that "God still holds the Jews most dear." Dialogue aimed at mutual understanding and respect is strongly recommended, and the idea of collective Jewish guilt for the death of Jesus is officially repudiated. His passion "cannot be charged against all Jews without distinction, then alive or alive today." This people "should not be presented as rejected or accursed by God, as if this follows from the Holy Scriptures." The Church does indeed have an obligation "to proclaim the cross of Christ, as the sign of God's all-embracing love and as the fountain from which every grace flows," but "we cannot truly call on God the Father of all, if we refuse to treat any man in a brotherly way." The Church therefore rejects discrimination of any kind, or harassment of any man on the basis of race, color, condition of life, or religion.

This same attitude is reflected in the *Declaration on Religious Freedom (Dignitatis Humanae)* of December 7, 1965, wherein the right of the human person to religious freedom, and man's obligation to follow his conscience, especially in religion, is unequivocally asserted.

Vatican II is now history, but it has stirred the Church to great activity. During the pontificate of Paul VI, meetings of an International Liaison Committee between the Catholic Church and world Judaism were held. Paul also established a Commission for Religious Relations with the Jews, which on December 1, 1974 issued its *Guidelines for Implementing the Conciliar Declaration "Nostra Aetate."* It recommended continued dialogue, and on-going "purification" of both Christian and Jewish literature of remarks unfavorable to the other, joint social action, and, most of all, appreciation of both the ancient and the Christian experience of God.

As Archbishop of Krakow, the present Pope John Paul II had courageously defended and assisted many Jews as well as others to whom human rights were being denied. When in a special audience on March 12, 1979 he met the representatives of world Jewish Organizations he was greeted with the words of the ancient Chronicler: "Peace, peace be to you, and peace to your helper!" (1 Chr 12:18). In response he noted the serious and sustained effort being made by the Roman Catholic Church to improve Jewish-Christian relations; continuing dialogue and understanding were slowly replacing monologue and suspicion. He again stressed the point that anti-Semitism and discrimination are contrary to the very spirit of Christianity. Quoting from the *Nostra Aetate*, the *Dignitatis Humanae*, and the *Guidelines*, he invoked God's help to bring about further reconciliation and love between the Christian and Jewish communities. Finally, he concluded his address with the words: "Peace be with you. Shalom. Shalom." The representatives went away with the precious conviction that genuine Christian love and friendship are pulsing strongly in the heart of the Church. The representatives were deeply moved and reassured by the words of a Polish Pope. Kindness and truth, justice and peace, had met and embraced (cf. Ps 85:11–12).

Assessing the Guilt

There have been many famous trials in history, but others pale into insignificance when compared with that of Jesus. More than any other, and with far less reason, he was the victim of judicial murder. How shall the guilt for his death be assigned? Obviously, the blame for it must be widely distributed.

The key figure in this miscarriage of justice is Judas, without whom there might not have been a trial. Pilate cannot be exonerated, for he had quickly perceived that the trial was uncalled for. Yet for all his bluster, he lacked moral courage and bowed under pressure giving the order to crucify an innocent man.

Crucifixion was a Roman form of punishment, and Jesus was executed upon a cross. Was he executed as a political rebel, as the inscription over the cross seems to indicate ("The King of the Jews" Mk 15:26)? Was he a guerilla leader of the Zealot type? No. The cleansing of the Temple and Jesus' "triumphal" entry into Jerusalem are poor support for such a charge, and there are basic differences between Jesus and the Zealots. With his bad administrative record, Pilate was an easy target for pressure. But was he alone responsible? It has been argued that if Jesus had been put to death by his own people, it would have been by one of the forms of capital punishment sanctioned by the Mishnah: stoning, strangling, or burning. Aside from the fact that the Mishnah was not at this time formally put together, there is the view—widely held—that the Jewish leaders were not allowed the right to impose capital punishment—the *jus gladii*. Rome jealously reserved that right to herself, which explains why Pilate enters the picture at all.

There were, to be sure, sporadic outbursts of violence despite Roman vigilance (for example, the stoning of Stephen), but in general it can be maintained that the Romans reserved the power of capital punishment. Indeed, Pilate extracted from the crowd the painful admission, "It is not lawful for us to put anyone to death" (Jn 18:21).

The Roman soldiers assigned to a routine task incurred no sin or guilt in the crucifixion of Jesus.

Pilate, Rome's representative of law and order, should not be saddled with all responsibility of the death of Jesus, but he cannot be absolved of all blame. What of "the Jews?"

The term, "the Jews," appears some sixty times in the Fourth Gospel. John wrote—this should be noted—long after the distinction between the various sects of Judaism had disappeared, and the use of this blanket term was adopted to make things easier for his readers. But John did not intend to include in it all Jews alive at the time. Many of these lived abroad, in a diaspora that extended far to the East and South and West. It was a diaspora that had come into being six centuries *before* the time of Christ, and thus is *not* the result of a supposed divine curse incurred by the death of Jesus (*pace* the myth of The Wandering Jew). None of those Jews, nor those of succeeding generations, had any part in Jesus' death, so all of them were and are innocent of guilt. Nor were all of those who lived in Palestine/Israel, all guilty, for among them were Jesus' own mother, John and the other apostles, and many followers and friends.

According to the context of time and space, "the Jews," in a pejorative sense, must refer only to "the leaders of the Jews," or "those who were opposed to him." By no means were all "the Jews" of Jesus' time spiritually or morally bankrupt. In the bosom of Israel there were, among the Scribes and Pharisees and others, many earnest seekers of God's will and kingdom.

Why were the high priests, the leaders of the people, so violently opposed to Jesus? The gospel is our only source for this period, and it suggests envy and jealousy as the reason. When one of them muttered, "The whole world has gone after him" (Jn 12:19), he revealed the smouldering depths of their resentment. Jesus was tried (and convicted?) on two counts: his claim to be the Messiah, and on the score that he was a false prophet ("He has made himself the Son of God" Jn 19:7). In the Roman court, the charge became one of treason, punishable by death.

What can be said of "the crowd" which played its part in the proceedings? At passover time, there was a great influx of pilgrims into the Holy City, but few of these would have had much knowledge about Christ and his teachings. The crowd that clamored for Jesus' death must have been relatively small in number, a hundred perhaps. The word "mob" derives from the Latin *turba mobilis*. It was volatile; under proper manipulation, crowds can easily be stirred to violence. In this case, the priestly leaders, invested with prestige and authority, would have had little difficulty in arousing the people. The very narrowness of the Jerusalem streets contributes even today to an easy communication of excitement.

Annas and Caiaphas, then, were chiefly responsible for the death of Jesus. The sons and daughters of Israel should not be punished for the sins of their ancestors. As Ezekiel said, "The son shall not suffer for the iniquity of the father . . . The soul that sins shall die" (18:20).

The Bible speaks forcefully to men of every age. Nowhere does it countenance self-deception (that is, a denial of one's sin), or self-righteousness (that is, seeing sin only in other people). All men are sinners, and Jesus, the Savior of all, died for our sins. As he was being nailed to the cross on Calvary, he prayed, "Father, forgive them . . ." (Lk 23:24). The words imply that there was something to be forgiven, that there was a need for pardon. They also reveal something that stirs the heart of every sinner, namely, that God is forgiving and more than willing to pardon his beloved but errant children.

The God of Abraham, Isaac, and Jacob has not rejected his people, as Paul assures us (Rom 9:25). There will come a day, in God's own time, when Christian and Jew will together and side by side give glory to God (cf. Zeph 3:9 and Rom 9–11). Until then, there remains for us to ponder the great mystery of God and his love. As Paul said to the Romans:

There is a deep truth here, my brothers, of which I want you to take account, so that you may not be complacent. Blindness has come on part of Israel until the full number of Gentiles enter in . . . If their rejection [of Jesus] has meant the reconciliation of the world, what will their acceptance mean! . . . O the depth of the riches and wisdom and knowledge of God! How unsearchable are his judgments, and how inscrutable his ways!" (Rom 11:25, 15, 33).

The Tomb of Christ

Men invariably erect monuments upon scenes where other men have performed heroic deeds and won great victories. It would be surprising if no monument had ever been reared upon the most famous sites of them all: Calvary, and the tomb of Christ. Indeed many monuments have succeeded each other over these two spots. Here, in brief résumé, is their history.

From April 7, 30 A.D., when Jesus died, to 70 A.D. when the Romans took Jerusalem and reduced it to ruins, no buildings marked the site of Calvary or of the Resurrection. This cannot be interpreted to mean that these places were not known or venerated; circumstances such as the poverty and small number of the Christians of that period are sufficient to explain the lack. A second Jewish revolt, launched under Simeon ben Koseba, lasted from 132 to 135, and proved to be as unsuccessful as the revolt of 66–70. This time, however, the Romans determined to make an object lesson of the city. Upon Hadrian's command, Roman engineers filled in the valleys and levelled the space which had once harbored both Calvary and the tomb, and made a huge forum. The city was constructed along Roman lines and given a new name. It was to be known as Aelia Capitolina for almost two centuries. In this colonial city there were many temples in honor of the pagan gods. Over the place where Jesus had been buried, the Romans built an idol of Jupiter; over Calvary, they erected a marble statue of Venus. Somewhere in the forum was a statue of the goddess mother Juno, and in the temple area, one of the emperor himself.

By putting up these temples to Jupiter and Venus where they did, the Romans were quite unintentionally pinpointing for future generations the exact locations of Calvary and of the tomb. ·Fathers telling their sons the story of the redemption would not fail to point out to them where exactly Jesus had died, and where he rose from the dead. The spots were clearly marked. When Constantine, a Christian emperor, came to the throne, he set about honoring the holy places. First, he demolished Hadrian's capitol; once rock level was reached beneath the forum, Calvary and the tomb were easily identifiable. The emperor then isolated the sepulchre from the non-essential rock surrounding it and, in the level space thus gained, he built a circular domed-church which was later given the name of *Anastasis*, or Resurrection. The area around Calvary was at this time also trimmed down, so as to emphasize it. When Constantine finished, the top of Calvary was some twelve to fourteen feet above that of the sepulchre floor. This section of the church, joined to the Anastasis by an atrium, was called the *Ecclesia ad Golgatha*.

Constantine's magnificant basilica, executed with all the wealth and technical skill of a great empire behind it, was dedicated in 335 A.D. It stood as Christianity's tribute and witness to the faith until its destruction in 615 at the hands of the Persians. The work of reconstruction which was soon begun came to a halt in 638 when the Holy Land fell under Moslem rule. An earthquake in 746 further damaged the edifice; repairs were not permitted. The lot of Christians was improved thanks to negotiations carried through by Charlemagne (d. 814), but the respite was brief. Climaxing a century of riot and anarchy, the Holy Sepulchre was, in 1009 A.D., literally broken into tiny bits by hammers at the command of Caliph Hakim. Yet Christians restored the sepulchre by 1048. After the capture of Jerusalem by the Crusaders (1099), a new and imposing basilica was begun; it was consecrated on July 15, 1149. It is this structure which the modern visitor to Jerusalem sees, although earthquakes, fires, neglect, and various amateurish repairs and changes (for example, the kiosk which now covers the restored tomb was put up in 1810), have combined to render the once imposing Frankish church all but unrecognizable. Mutilated, stripped of its decorations, the Church of the Resurrection and of Golgotha is today almost in ruins, and gives but a feeble impression of its former splendor.

The shabby condition of the Church of the Resurrection, which has persisted since the Crusaders were driven out of Palestine, has in times past led men to look for a more dignified place as a fit location for Calvary and the Sepulchre.

It may be of interest to catalogue here the story of the so-called Garden Tomb.

In a garden located along the road to Nablus, which runs northward from the Damascus Gate in Jerusalem, a cave was discovered in 1867. On the wall of the cave, someone had painted a cross in red, flanked by an *alpha* and an *omega*. The diggings here were continued on into 1870, by which time it was clear that the cave had once been used as a tomb. Smudges caused by oil-lamps placed in niches along the wall were interpreted with some eagerness as an indication that the tomb may have once been the site of a cult, although proof was lacking.

The matter rested until 1883, when Jerusalem was visited by the famous Englishman, General Charles "Chinese" Gordon (1833–85). As the story goes, Gordon, who was soon to achieve great renown for his gallant defense at Khartoum in the Sudan, was one day walking atop the north wall of Jerusalem when his eye fell upon an abandoned quarry across the road. His impressions, written as L. H. Vincent observes, with "the enthusiasm of a neophite and the decisiveness of a strategist," were later published (1885) in the pages of the *Quarterly Statement* of the Palestine Exploration Fund. A constant reader of the Bible, Gordon was convinced that Bezetha (which he called "Skull Hill") was the real Calvary. The next and logical step was to find the tomb of Christ. There is some question whether Gordon actually thought the Garden Tomb was the tomb of Christ, but he endorsed the general vicinity.

It was not long before men were enthusiastically referring to the Garden Tomb and Skull Hill as the real Tomb and Calvary. In 1882 the French Dominicans had acquired the adjacent property north of the Garden Tomb. In the course of the extensive excavations they conducted on the site of the martyrdom of St. Stephen, there came to light, in May, 1889, in what is now the courtyard of the graceful basilica there, a tomb upon which the following inscription could be read: "The private tomb of the deacon, Nonnus Onesimus, of the church of the Resurrection of Christ and of this monastery."

From the moment this news was bruited about Jerusalem, the star of Gordon's Tomb began to glow strongly. This was due to a total disregard for fact, unrestrained imagination, and the complete unleashing of the emotions—all discernible in certain American and English "religious" publications which espoused the cause of the Garden Tomb.

The main argument in favor of the Garden Tomb lies rather in the Onesimus' inscription. Contrary to the garbled version of it which appeared in the news of the day, the inscription did *not* say that Onesimus (or Nonnus *and* Onesimus) was "buried close to his Lord;" it simply stated that he was "of the Church of the Resurrection of Christ." This phrase means only that Nonnus Onesimus, who belonged to the monastery of St. Stephen, had exercised diaconal functions at the Church of the *Anastasis*, an honor so singular that it was recorded on his tomb. Other examples of the same honorific title, it may be added, have been found elsewhere in the Jerusalem area.

All sciences suffer periodically from a sensation-loving press, and even the most staid of publications may on occasion be quite carried away. A case in point is the *London Times* of July 24, 1924, which published the headline: *Garden Tomb. New Jerusalem Discovery. Shrine Stone and its Meaning.* The stone in question was reverently declared to be a model of Hadrian's second century temple to Venus. Actually, the stone was one of many which a Danish sculptor had carved some fifteen years before while he worked as caretaker of the Garden Tomb. In far-off London, however, the stone was taken as conclusive proof of the authenticity of the Garden Tomb.

From the very first, competent archeologists have rejected all claims made for the Garden Tomb. R.A.F. Macalister wrote in the *Quarterly Statement,* "Nothing whatever can be said in favor of the tomb." Scholarly Charles Clermont-Ganneau expressed his astonishment that anyone should take Gordon's fantasies seriously. When *The Times* published the story of the shrine stone, P. Vincent of the Ecole Biblique et Archéologique Française de Jérusalem wrote a devastating article in the *Revue biblique,* entitled "Garden Tomb, Histoire d'un mythe." Yet only ten years after that, the Director of the Department of Antiquities in Palestine, Mr. Ernest Tatham Richmond, felt obliged to demonstrate again the complete falsity of the claims made for the Garden Tomb. More recently still, M. André Parrot, curator of the French National Museums and famed for his work on the Mari Tablets, noted the unanimity of informed opinion against the Gardent Tomb. His concluding words are:

"I have dealt with it [the Garden Tomb] here simply because it was necessary to say again, in the most categorical terms, that nothing was ever more certain than that the Garden Tomb is a myth. One hopes that no sensible person will ever again be misled by it."

Alas, archeological ghosts, once released, are exceedingly difficult to recapture and bind in chains. It is a melancholy commentary on human nature to have to record that in this age of archeological enlightenment, and despite repeated exposures, the Garden Tomb still has its devotees. They can be seen wending their way, each Easter morning, up the lane which leads to a funerary complex which *may* date from the Herodian period, and which *certainly* contains graves and crosses of the fifth and sixth centuries A.D. But that is all. The site of the tomb of Christ is still the traditional one—in the Church of the Holy Sepulchre.

INDEX

232.96   Murphy,
M978d   Days of glory.   202

DATE DUE	BORROWER'S NAME	ROOM NUMBER
3-14-94	Sr. Jenny	
	Sr. Irene	

Murphy   202